The Ocean Queen

Hilary Wyatt

Sceptre Publications

COPYRIGHT

The right of Hilary J. Wyatt to be identified as the author of this work has been asserted by her in accordance with the Copyright, Designs and Patents Act 1988. All rights reserved. No part of this publication may be reproduced, stored in a retrieval system or transmitted in any form without the prior written consent of the author, nor be otherwise circulated in any form of binding or cover other than that in which it is published and without a similar condition being imposed on the subsequent purchaser.

Copyright Hilary J. Wyatt 2024

Published by Sceptre Publications, 2024
Design by Ben Woodcraft Designs
ISBN: 9781838309442. Printed in the UK

I dedicate this book to George & Dereen
Richardson's 3 great grandchildren, Ethan, Mila,
& Sydney Georgina - and Edward Richardson
(1998 – 2023 see last page)

Contents

PREFACE		6
CHAPTER 1	**THE OCEAN QUEEN**	9
CHAPTER 2	**A SMALL HAMLET BECOMES A THRIVING TOWN**	13
CHAPTER 3	**JAMES AND DOROTHY IN SEAHAM HARBOUR**	17
CHAPTER 4	**SEAHAM HARBOUR AT THE TURN OF THE 20TH CENTURY**	33
CHAPTER 5	**THE GENERAL STRIKE & ERNEST'S ADVENTURES IN THE US OF A**	39
CHAPTER 6	**THE HUGUENOTS**	53
CHAPTER 7	**GEORGE AND MARY**	59
CHAPTER 8	**ERNEST AND RACHEL**	67
CHAPTER 9	**GEORGE AND DEREEN**	73
CHAPTER 10	**GEORGE AND DEREEN AND THE 2ND WORLD WAR**	83
CHAPTER 11	**GEORGE AND DEREEN AND FAMILY LIFE**	113
CHAPTER 12	**MEMORIES OF THE NORTH EAST AND RELATIVES**	117
CHAPTER 13	**HOPE AND HEARTACHE**	129
CHAPTER 14	**MY SPIRITUAL JOURNEY**	161
CHAPTER 15	**CAN IT REALLY BE TRUE?**	171
CHAPTER 16	**WHAT IF?**	179
CHAPTER 17	**TINKER, TAILOR, SOLDIER, SAILOR**	181
BIBLIOGRAPHY		185
APPENDIX AND NOTES		189

OCEAN QUEEN

PREFACE

This book starts with a ship in the 19th century and ends with a ship in the 20th century.

There is a book which could be written about every family. Whether we are interested in our family's history or not, the fact is, we are all shaped by the past, and decisions made by family members of previous generations. We owe our very existence to where they chose to live, whom they chose to marry and sometimes even small, seemingly insignificant decisions can have long-reaching effects.

Researching family history has become a popular pastime. Programmes on television such as "Who do you think you are?" may have fuelled people's interest or it could be that the programme was produced in response to interest already present.

There are those who research their family history in the hope of finding an illustrious personage. It is human nature to want to come from "good stock" but for every illustrious personage one might find, there will be the not-so-illustrious!

As we ponder over past generations of our family, the ones we have known and those who died before we were born, it is good to be inspired by the good and learn from the mistakes of the past. Families are so very important. The fabric of a nation disintegrates when families fall apart.

The old chestnut of how much of who we are is nurture or nature still continues to fascinate many. We cannot get away from the fact that the decisions of past generations have had a huge impact on our lives just as the culture we have grown up with affects our worldview, but in the end, it is up to each one of us, how we live our lives. However, as John Donne wrote, "No man is an island" and how we live doesn't just affect ourselves but our children, our children's children, our friends and those we come into contact with. Just as previous generations have impacted our lives, we cannot escape the fact that how we live our lives will impact future generations of our family. I am inviting you to come on a journey with me - a journey of a family's history. They say that life is often stranger than fiction and in following two particular family lines, this is certainly the case.

1

THE OCEAN QUEEN

Echoes of the past come flooding through my mind as I gaze at the ancient pair of binoculars in my hands. They are one of those objects that have always been in my life and hold a myriad of memories. Memories of using them on holiday to look at boats out at sea, memories of my mother looking through them and getting excited when spotting an unusual bird in our garden, but most of all memories of being told the story of the man who had first owned them! Some of his story my mother recounted to me, but much more, I was to find out later.

The story begins on a cold, dark day in Norfolk on Friday, October 29th in the year 1880. By the afternoon, a storm was raging and to be out at sea off Holkham Beach was not a good place to be! The conditions were treacherous! The Wells lifeboat, Eliza Adams had already gone to the aid of a brig called Sharon's Rose saving the crew of 7, when a second ship was seen flying a distress signal.

The brig, Ocean Queen was riding at anchor in that very heavy sea, her sails ripped to shreds in the violent wind. The Eliza Adams was towed to the Harbour entrance by the steam tug Promise and released around half a mile from the Ocean Queen at about 3:30 p.m. By now, Ocean Queen had parted its cable and had been driven onto the East Sands by the high winds. With the vessel aground on the Lee shore, the lifeboat could not be of any assistance, so the order was given to set sails to return to the harbour.

Around a quarter of an hour later, a large sea broke over the lifeboat, capsizing her and driving her mast into the sand, preventing the lifeboat from self-righting. Eleven of the crew of thirteen lost their lives, leaving ten widows and twenty-eight children. The wreck of the Ocean Queen dried out as the tide ebbed that evening and Captain Charles Sinden and his crew were able to walk safely to the shore.

1880 was a very sad year for Dorothy Saunders, the owner of the Ocean Queen who had only recently lost her husband, James to tuberculosis and now had to bear the news of this awful loss of life which involved the Ocean Queen plus the loss of their ship. Dorothy was my great, great, grandmother and her husband, James my great, great, grandfather, the original owner of the binoculars!

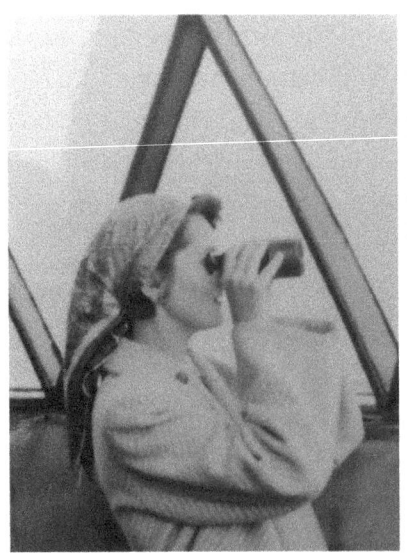 

JAMES' GREAT-GRANDDAUGHTER, DEREEN USING HIS BINOCULARS

BOOKLET ISSUED IN 2005 COMMEMORATING THE DISASTER OF THE ELIZA ADAMS.

2

A SMALL HAMLET BECOMES A THRIVING TOWN

James and Dorothy Saunders lived in Seaham Harbour, a town on the northeast coast of England. The small ancient hamlet of Seaham with its beautiful 11th-century church of Saint Mary's had a population of just 22 in 1801. It would have remained an inconspicuous little place had it not been for a certain Lord of the Manor at that time who in 1792 replaced the Manor house with a much grander one called Seaham Hall. Sir Ralph Milbanke MP was a man with a vision, a vision which many thought ridiculous. The vision was to see a harbour at a rocky inlet on the coast nearby at Dalden Ness. This could be used to take coals from the newly sunk Hetton Colliery. Most harbours are built into a bay, but if there was to be a harbour at Dalden Ness, it would need to be hewn out of the cliffs. In 1820 Sir Ralph commissioned the eminent engineer William Chapman to draw up plans. Unfortunately, Sir Ralph never saw his vision materialise during his time in Seaham. He had to abandon the plan the following year as his fortune had taken a downward turn, not helped by the large dowry he'd had to pay on his daughter Isabella's marriage to Lord Byron In 1815. In 1821, he sold Seaham Hall and its estates to Lord Charles Stewart who was soon to become the 3rd Marquis of Londonderry.

SEAHAM HALL

LORD LONDONDERRY

Lord Londonderry saw that Sir Ralph's vision made economic sense but the idea was still not held to be viable as 30 ships had foundered off the rocky coast in that area in 1824. Lord Londonderry, however, sought opinions from two more eminent engineers - Telford and Rennie. He then decided to retain Will Chapman as an engineer for the project. Lord Londonderry was to be the man who would make Sir Ralph's vision become a reality!

THE MAKING OF THE HARBOUR AND THE TOWN

Work began in September 1828. The first stage was completed in July 1831 and the whole project was completed in 1835 at a cost of £165,000. William Chapman, who died not long after the completion of the North Dock in 1832, wrote that there was "no instance of a private harbour being constructed with such rapidity and to such an extent as the present harbour has been."

In 1843 Dalden Ness was renamed Seaham Harbour. Since the completion of the harbour in less than a decade, the little hamlet of Seaham had become a thriving town bringing in up to 50 sailing collier ships daily which supplied London and Eastern towns with coal for industry and domestic use.

THE WORLD COMES TO SEAHAM HARBOUR

After the harbour was built, it brought an influx of people taking advantage of the opportunities for the many businesses needed to support the ship building and needs of the growing population. People came to settle from other parts of Britain and Ireland and ships brought the world to Seaham Harbour. The ships came from different places in the U.K. and in later times from abroad but also had a variety of nationalities among the crew. Some of the crew were from Scotland, Shetland and the Orkneys, Ireland, Wales, Jersey, Guernsey, Belgium, Germany, USA, Holland, France, Russia, Finland, Sierra Leone, Jamaica, Australia, Gibraltar, Sweden, Norway, Denmark and Italy.

In July 1855, The Londonderry Sunderland and Seaham Railway was completed. It cost £50,000 and not only provided valuable access to the Sunderland docks for the coal trade but was also a passenger railway with stations at Seaham Colliery and Ryhope. The entire journey from Seaham Harbour to Sunderland took only 15 minutes.

3

JAMES AND DOROTHY IN SEAHAM

With the prospect of work, Seaham Harbour attracted people from all over the North East and much further afield as has been stated in the previous chapter. James Saunders was born in Wapping, Middlesex, which had the main entrance to the London docks in 1824, but according to his daughter-in-law, Isabella, the family originated from Cornwall. This was entirely possible as James's father, Charles was a mariner and as such tended to be more geographically mobile than most. According to Fred Cooper, in his book called *The Hole in the Wall*, there was an "influx of people from Cornwall, Essex, Norfolk and other rural counties seeking work," as well as people from the neighbouring counties of Durham and Northumberland. There was actually a street in Seaham called Cornish Street. People were also attracted to nearby Sunderland which boasted the justifiable claim of being the largest ship-building town in the world!

James's father, Charles found his teenage son an apprenticeship in Seaham Harbour. James lodged with Charles and Alice Merchant in North Railway Street, as found in an 1841 census. His apprenticeship at that time is listed as ship's carpenter, but he went on to be apprenticed to ship owner Thomas Bell in 1842 and later became a Master Mariner.

MARRIAGE, THE GOLD RUSH AND BABIES

On December the 14th 1849, James age 25 married 27 year-old Dorothy Wylam who was born in Washington, County Durham.

Her father William Wylam was a blacksmith. Their marriage took place in Shadforth Church, County Durham, which was presumably in the parish where Dorothy had been living, as it was traditional to get married in the bride's home church.

James and Dorothy are not listed in the 1851 census and it has been passed down the generations that they went to a gold rush so presumably this was the year they sailed off together to pan for gold. According to cousin Geoff Saunders, it must have been the Australian Gold Rush as their marriage in December 1849 rules out the gold rush in the States. The year 1851 was quite a year for Australia. In February a man named Hargreaves discovered gold near Bathurst, New South Wales.

Word got around and within a week of this discovery 400 people came panning for gold and by June that number had increased to 2000. Later that year in August, James Reagan and John Dunlop discovered the richest gold field that the world has ever seen in a place the Aborigines called Bala Arat which is now the city of Ballarat. Finally, in September a lady called Margaret Kennedy discovered the Bendigo goldfields. Over the next decade, a third of the world's gold came from Australia.

Life was not easy for those early gold diggers. The work was hard, living conditions cramped (later guesthouses were set up) and because the alluvial mining muddied the nice clean creek water, drinking water was hard to find. Often freshwater was carted into the diggings and was sold by the bucketful. Fresh fruit and vegetables were scarce and expensive. Many people died of dysentery or typhoid.

Not long after they came back Dorothy was pregnant with their first child whom they named James Charles after his father and grandfather. Tragically, their baby only survived 6 days. It was to be six years later in 1857 before their only surviving child, Charles was born in Seaham Harbour.

JAMES BECOMES A MASTER MARINER

We do not know for certain if they were successful in finding any gold but something had to finance the ships which James subsequently purchased. It does not appear from the fact that James' father, whose occupation was a mariner, or Dorothy's father whose occupation was a blacksmith, that either family would have been able to give them the sort of money to be able to finance several ships, the cost of which would have run into several thousand pounds – a huge sum in those days!

In the 1861 census, James is found living with Dorothy and their three-year-old son Charles in Francis Street, Seaham Harbour. James's occupation is still a ship's carpenter, the same trade he was in as a teenage apprentice in 1841. However, by 1864 he had become a Master Mariner of the James Chadwick and was to purchase ships of his own. One can only presume that he had money from the gold rush which was the impetus for him becoming a Master Mariner and buying his own ships.

JAMES BECOMES A SHIPOWNER

The latter part of the 1850s, through into the 1860s saw a satisfying time for Charles and Dorothy when all their plans and dreams were coming to pass. They had their little healthy son, Charles, James had become a Master Mariner and then a ship-owner and also a property owner, owning several houses in Adolphus Street, Seaham Harbour. Times were very good for the little family. According to an article in a newspaper, Charles Saunders, his grandson (and the author's great uncle), James owned three ships, the Ocean Queen, Sceptre and Bradford and part-owned The James Chadwick. However, there is no record of him part owning the James Chadwick, only the record of him being a Master Mariner on that ship.

RECEIPTS BELONGING TO JAMES

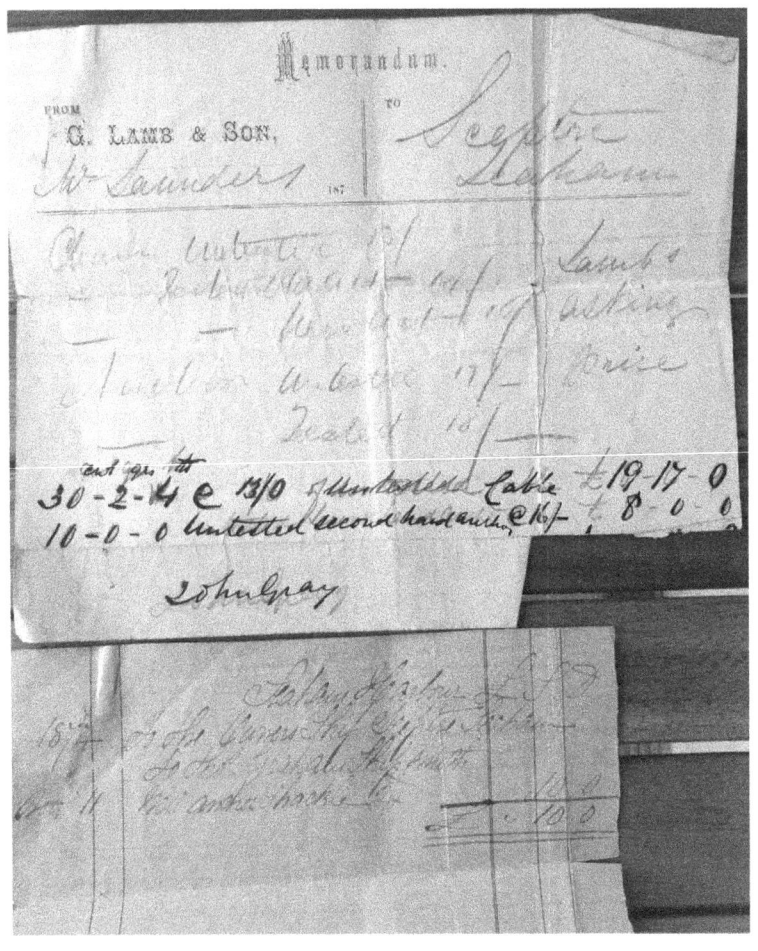

RECEIPT BELONGING TO JAMES

Nov 23 / 74

Mr T Davison
Sir
I inclose the ac-
count of the Sceptre
chain and anchor

	£	s	d
1 One Shakell		10	
Anchor an	9	..	..
45 fathem chane	24	8	4
Getting on bor	..	8	..

RECEIPT BELONGING TO JAMES

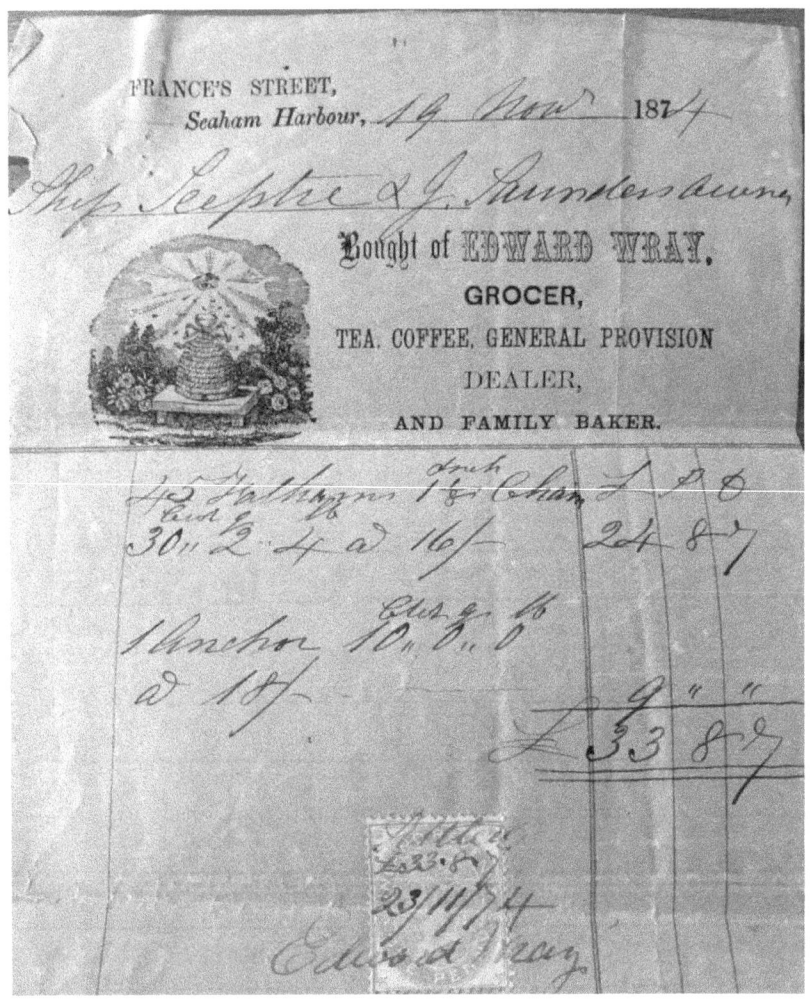

SUNDERLAND - birthplace of the Saxon scholar, The Venerable Bede, the most learned Englishman of his age. Both the Ocean Queen and Sceptre were built in nearby Sunderland which in 1851 boasted around 70 shipbuilders and for many years was the biggest shipbuilding town in the world. This achievement was earned through the hard work and skill of generations of Sunderland shipbuilders. The great names of Pile, Doxford, Thompson, Austin, Pickersgill, Laing, Short and Bartram are still remembered as men of genius who established the industry on the banks of the river Wear. They founded the shipyard firms that survived world wars, the Depression and many changes in the industry to launch some of the finest ships ever constructed. These ships were built by shipwrights, caulkers, platers and welders, plus a lot more skilled crafts whose craftmanship was the envy of the world. At the peak of shipbuilding in Sunderland there were sometimes 3 launches in an hour. Shipbuilding started in Sunderland more than 600 years ago and coal was sent to London as early as 1396. In addition to coal, there has been a large general cargo trade of both imports and exports. The old Wearmouth bridge which was built and opened in 1796 was for many years the largest single-span iron bridge in the world. It was replaced in 1929 and opened by George VI when he was Duke of York. (The end of shipbuilding on the Wear in the 1980s saw the closure of some of the most up-to-date facilities in the country).

THE RIVER WEAR AT SUNDERLAND (From a painting by K W Burton)

LIFE ON THE OCEAN WAVE WAS HARD – FORTUNES MADE AND LOST

Unfortunately, things were often uncertain during James and Dorothy's times where ships were involved.

Fred Cooper wrote in his book *A Hole in the Wall*, "Fortunes were often made and lost. Many voyages were very profitable but if a ship was not insured, foundered and was lost at sea, those ship-owners risked not only the value of the cargo but also the capital used to purchase the ship. Sailing ships regularly arrived at ports with loss of rigging, anchor and chains, sprung leaks with all hands to the pumps for hours or even days on end, collisions at sea, men overboard and also ships were abandoned in heavy seas."

THE WRITING ON THE WALL

1871 was the year when circumstances took a downward turn for James and Dorothy. James's ship Sceptre, his brigantine built by JM Gales at South Hylton Sunderland in 1836 was involved in a collision with a ship called the Mary and Ann, in the English Channel one-and-a-half miles off the coast of Deal. She was carrying coal. We don't know if James was insured but the answer is probably not, in view of his later activities.

He must have also known that the writing was on the wall as far as the viability of sailing ships. There were already signs that steamships were the way forward. As early as 1852 the steamer "John Bowes" was launched in Jarrow. She cost 10,000 pounds - a huge sum in those days especially when compared with a sailing ship which cost around 1000 pounds. However, on her first voyage, loaded with 650 tons of coal, she took only four days to reach London and back. She had done as much work in less than a week from the North East as a sailing vessel would have done in two months!

James must have been a desperate man as he faced the expense of repairing the Sceptre plus the loss of revenue from trade while the repairs were in progress and the looming spectre of the new steamships threatening to eliminate his livelihood and all that he had spent his life working for.

The Mercantile Shipping Gazette dated 26th of July 1876 reveals his response to this situation. This publication contained information regarding a court case James had been involved in. It was regarding an alleged sale of "Sceptre" by James to a Belgium owner. It was found that in fact James still owned the ship and he had made up the sale to avoid registration and inspection fees and excise duties. There was a board of trade inquiry and James's ship was confiscated.

JAMES DIES

More sadness was to follow for the family. After just a few years in 1879, James became ill with tuberculosis. 1879 was a very cold year, even during the summer months and as the year drew to a close, it was bitterly cold. December was the coldest month of the 19th century and the temperature continued to be very low into January. Despite these conditions, there was a lack of rain causing a notable drought from October to January. Queen Victoria had now been on the throne for over forty years and Benjamin Disraeli was prime minister. The year drew to a close with a tragic accident. On December 28th, a train from Burntisland to Dundee was passing over the Tay bridge during a violent storm when the bridge collapsed and people were plunged into the water below. An estimated 75 people lost their lives. Harry Watts, an ancestor of my cousin Geoffrey Saunders (on his mother's side) was one of the divers who helped recover some of the bodies.

HARRY WATTS 1826 – 1913

Harry also recovered a log boat from the River Wear which is reckoned to be about 700 years old and can be viewed at Sunderland Museum. Between 1839 and 1892 he saved over 36 people from drowning and assisted in the rescue of 120 as a member of Sunderland Lifeboat and Life Brigade Services. Harry (Henry) was born in the East End of Sunderland on the 15th of June 1826. When he was 14 he became apprentice on the brig "Lena "and went to sea. From 1847 he had shore based jobs including ships rigger but returned to sea in 1852. In 1857, after a heavy drinking session that nearly killed him, he became a Christian which he considered the most important event in his life. In 1861 he became a diver for the River Wear Commissioners. After meeting him, the industrialist and philanthropist Andrew Carnegie from the USA described him as "The bravest man I have ever met" and commented, " I have today been introduced to a man who has, I think the most ideal character of any man living on the face of the earth. You should never let the memory of this Sunderland man die."

The year 1880 dawned. James was still battling tuberculosis. As Spring beckoned, the weather began to improve, but by March James's battle came to an end when on Wednesday, March the 10th he finally breathed his last breath. On his death certificate, it is recorded he suffered for nine months four days and six hours. I imagine Dorothy, who was to become matron of the Seaham Infirmary kept a record of this! The personal sadness for Dorothy and Charles must have been hard to bear especially watching James's suffering over such a long period, but things were about to get even worse for the whole community.

TRAGEDY FOR THE WHOLE TOWN

Later that year of 1880 on Wednesday September 8th at twenty past two in the morning, there was a major explosion In the mine. 164 men and boys were killed. There must have been hardly a family in Seaham who had not lost a loved one

- a husband, father, son, grandson, brother or nephew. Sorrow and grief must have permeated the air in that little town and they also had to cope with the ensuing poverty and deprivation that transpired from this tragedy.

Charles aged 23 was still living with his mother Dorothy. Financially they were provided for, as Charles had a job as an engine fitter at Seaham Harbour Engine Works and they had one ship left - the Ocean Queen until that fateful day on Friday, October the 29th as described in the first chapter of this book. After such a disastrous start to the decade, Dorothy and Charles's life began to improve during the 1880s. Dorothy became matron of Seaham Infirmary and Charles, aged 25 married his sweetheart, Isabella Gray (born in Stockton) aged 20 in nearby Sunderland in 1882. Isabella quickly became pregnant with their first child and Dorothy's first grandchild. In January 1883, Isabella gave birth to a son whom they called James Charles (the same name as James and Dorothy's first child who died in infancy) after his father and grandfather. Unfortunately, tragedy struck again when the baby died. (In early 1889, another baby they called James was born to them who also died in infancy but finally in early 1893, ten years after the first James, Isabella gave birth to a third baby James who survived!)

In 1885 Charles and Isabella had the joy of the birth of their first daughter, Elizabeth and for Dorothy, Elizabeth was her first granddaughter. February the 25th 1887 saw the birth of Ernest at the Seaham Infirmary where his grandmother Dorothy was matron.

Ernest was my grandfather. I remember him telling me of his impression of Dorothy as a young child. He remembered going to see her at the Infirmary which to his young eyes was a rather foreboding place. (I must admit that I thought the same as a child when it was pointed out to me!) He described his grandmother as being a kind but rather proper lady. Although this is an impression from a very small child, this description does seem to fit Dorothy. She would have needed kindness and some steeliness to be able to do her job at the Infirmary where she would have had to nurse people with horrific injuries and diseases – a job she continued to do until her late sixties, and also to have gone panning for gold with her husband. That was a hard life and it was rare for a woman to be involved.

SEAHAM INFIRMARY

DOROTHY DIES

Charles and Isabella were to go on to parent four more of Dorothy's grandchildren, Bertie, James, Dorothy and Charles, but sadly she was not to see them. On Tuesday, November the 25th in the year 1890 Dorothy, aged 68 died of typhoid which she probably contracted while nursing seafarers.

Just two years after Dorothy's passing, 1892 brought severe hardship to the North East with the miner's strike. This strike was against the intention of the pit owners to reduce wages following a fall in the price of coal and coke. It started on the 9th of March and did not end until June 3rd. There were more than eighty thousand men out of work and many more thousands in related industries. Many hundreds of iron workers were laid off and all those related to the shipbuilding industry. Smokeless chimneys, cold furnaces and ships laid up signified the cost of the strike not only for the miners but for many others. There was no work and people were on the verge of starvation. The miners eventually went back to work but had to suffer reduced wages.

Dorothy's grandson and my grandfather, Ernest went on to marry Rachel Barker who was a bakeress in Seaham Harbour at the time of their marriage. Ernest was an interesting character who definitely inherited some of the drive and abilities of his grandfather, James Saunders and also was blessed with an amazing memory. In the next chapter, I will let him speak in his own words about Seaham Harbour at the beginning of the 1900s.

DOROTHY SAUNDERS NEE WYLAM

Charles and Isabella's family - Left to right, standing - Dorothy born in 1897 whose profession was a dressmaker, James born in 1893 whose profession was a pattern maker at Seaham Engineering Works, Bertie born in 1889 who died of war wounds in 1918, Ernest born in 1887 and Elizabeth born in 1885 whose profession was a music teacher. Seated - Isabella and Charles with little Charles born in 1901

4

SEAHAM HARBOUR AT THE TURN OF THE 20TH CENTURY

According to Fred Cooper, "The original harbour only accommodated vessels up to 1000 tons and larger ships had to use the port of Sunderland but in 1905, the completion of the extension of the South Dock by incorporating the dry harbour allowed ships of up to 5000 tons to use the port." (The name Seaham Harbour was changed in 1939 to be just "Seaham.")

In 1965, James and Dorothy Saunders' grandson, Ernest, my grandfather wrote down his memories of Seaham Harbour at the beginning of the 1900s. Ernest worked as a draftsman for Seaham Engineering Works and later after his adventures in the United States, he worked for Doxford's Shipbuilders in Sunderland as an engineer until the 1950s when he retired. As an engineer in shipbuilding, his job would have been to provide, manage and apply technical expertise in outfitting to the design, selection and testing of equipment for all ships under construction. I remember my cousin Jimmy who also worked with him saying that he was an exceptional engineer.

Doxford's Shipyard started building ships up river. William Doxford then moved to a site at Pallion in 1857 that would become the biggest yard on the Wear. In 1902 work began on transforming the berths and workshops and between 1905 and 1907 their output was greater than any other shipyard in the world. The 1970s saw another modernization with the "Cedarbank" being the first ship floated out of their new covered yard on May 26th 1976. At that time it was the biggest indoor shipyard in the world.

INDUSTRY IN SEAHAM HARBOUR

As a Seaham man, I remember Seaham Harbour at the turn of The century, when it was quite a smallish town, but a very busy one, with its many thriving industries. There were the bottle works, chemical works, foundry and engineering works. The latter works were the main industry at that time. It was Lord Londonderry's engine works employing many hundreds of men of all crafts and building locomotives, both passenger and goods type.

There are not many men left in Seaham who worked there. The manager of these works was a Mr George Hardy. I started as an apprentice in August 1901. This was the year when the then Lord Londonderry sold these works and all the rolling stock and his private railway which ran from Seaham to Sunderland. All employees could travel for two and a half pence return privileged tickets. These works were situated on the now derelict land just east of Dawdon railway crossing. A remnant of the machinery and plant was removed to a new factory on Foundry Road at the east end of Seaham.

Here, Mr George Hardy retired and was succeeded by Mr John Donavon from Sunderland who introduced a new industry building steam wagons. These vehicles were then in their infancy. This dynamic manager designed and built the first waggon from January 4th 1903 to June 26th 1903. There are still many men alive today (in 1965) who worked on these steam wagons and will remember the many grim experiences or breakdowns on the road in wintertime. There were three designs before they finally overcame their teething troubles. This manager left after about four years. His draughtsman Mr E.G. Allison of Sunderland stepped into his place and started to build petrol vehicles.

These were freak designs and were never a practical success. This factory was finally closed down after the end of the first war.

Next door to the above factory was the Seaham Foundry Company. The manager was Mr George Millar and his co-partner, Mr E. Rumfitt. It was quite a busy place making cast iron work of every description for marine engineering. It still exists but is managed by a Sunderland firm.

Also nearby was a timber yard owned by Mr Joseph Elgy JP. He built this business up to a high standard of efficiency. I believe it is still in his family.

Some 200 yards south of these factories was the Seaham Harbour Bottle Works employing hundreds of men and owned by Joseph Candlish. There must have been many millions of bottles made there and transported by sea to London in their own little steamer "Oakwell" which was lost in the first war. These works closed down some half a century ago.

There was also a brewery in Seaham. It went by the name of Chilton's Brewery. Head Brewer was Mr George Swan. He could make real beer in those days for three pence a pint. In the bottle works mentioned earlier, there must also have been many millions of gallons of Chilton's beer consumed for it was a very hot job in those days. Yes, Seaham Harbour in those far-off days was a happy and close-knit community.

COMMUNITY CELEBRATIONS

Seaham had its annual Flower Show held on the grounds of Lord Londonderry's Seaham Hall, now a hospital. (Now in the 21st century, it is an hotel). This event was quite the highlight of each year with cycle track racing and all the fun of the fair with Murphy's roundabouts etc. – as Albert Whelam would have sang, "There was a happy little wedding planned at the flower show!" I can still smell the coconuts, oil burners and all the smells that make up these happy events!

Another great annual event was the Inspection Day of the Seaham Volunteers when they marched up to the Drill Field to be inspected by Lord Londonderry. It was quite a stirring sight to see the volunteers with their uniforms and busbys marching with such precision and the gun batteries with their powerful horses, headed by their brass band. This day ended with The Volunteer's Ball held in the Drill Hall when his lordship led off the first dance.

Another annual event was the Cycle Parade held on a Sunday morning when thousands of cyclists paraded around the town ending up at Seaham Hall to receive a bottle of beer and a pie.

There was also an annual swimming Gala held in the docks and a Regatta out at sea with coal trimmers using their shovels oars. This event ceased after a disaster to a coble which overturned and some of the crew were drowned.

I often visit my old hometown which has now grown into quite a large place. I was born in the Seaham Infirmary 78 years ago where my grandmother Dorothy was matron. I notice that the Seaham Harbour Council has now vacated this building for new offices. Like all towns, the face of Seaham has changed for the better and will be better still in the future when all its

plans materialise.
I wish it well in these future days.
Ernest Saunders.

CHARLES SAUNDERS, ERNEST'S FATHER IS ON THE RIGHT OF THE MAN ON THE EXTREME LEFT WITH THE LARGE HAT.

5

THE GENERAL STRIKE AND ERNEST'S ADVENTURES IN THE US OF A.

The 1920s were dire years for many in the North East followed by the great depression of the first part of the 1930s. The orders for new ships had all but ceased. Doxford's Shipbuilders actually closed for several years. The pay was extremely low for many who were in work, especially for the miners who were part of the general strike of 1926 which impacted the whole area and industries associated with coal.

During this time, my grandfather Ernest decided to go in search of work in the United States. He intended to get established and bring his wife, Rachel and four children, Sid, Arthur, Gladys and Dereen over to settle there. My mother, Dereen was his youngest daughter and was only seven, nearly eight when her father left for the USA. If this plan had succeeded, my father would not have met my mother and our family and also my cousins' families would not exist.

The following is an account of his adventures in his own words which he wrote in his passport.

JAMES' GRANDSON ERNEST - THE PROMISE OF A BETTER FUTURE

This idea of mine to go and work in the US was born in my mind some 2 years before it came to reality. The germ was always there and I used to read about conditions in that country. The final decision came after I read a book on the findings of a British team of craftsmen union leaders who went out to research and see for themselves whether all the stories of working conditions and everyday life were true or just eye wash.

The Daily Mail organised and paid all expenses, paying each man a weekly wage, also their wives while they were away. They were in the USA for two weeks and were given the freedom to talk to any working people or executives during their visit. The result was that they found that everything previously published in British newspapers was true, that wages were very much higher and everyone had a much higher standard of living than the British workmen. One had to work efficiently and fast, but every craftsman in all trades had more machinery to help them to accomplish this.

The man that swept the floor or shop floor had his own home, car and bank account, telephone and every conceivable gadget in the home to make life easy. Yes, it might have been on the "Never, never" but he got three times the wages of a similar British craftsman. There was no room for loafers and passengers in factories - they were soon out. The aforementioned book published after this team returned to England was published for a mere 2 pence at a loss in order to try and wake up the sluggish British.

There have been many such teams who visited the US, especially since the last war, embracing every class of industry, farming, mining, etc and have returned with similar reports of the efficiency of everything in the USA.

THE US OF A, HERE I COME!

Therefore in early 1927, I made my first move and hunted up the American consul who put me under a sort of third-degree exam, filled in forms etc and then after a few weeks I had to report to the American consul in Liverpool where you were put through a rigid medical and questioning why you wanted to go to the US etc and I must have someone over there to stand bond for me. I had a cousin, Will Jubb who did this in an attorney's court – to cut a long story short I received a sailing date for October 29th 1927 on the Samaria.

I was 40 years of age but very fit and confident with every hope of one day having my dear wife and family with me out there, but man proposes and God disposes. After that terrible 1926 strike when I was working in Dawdon Colliery which I hated for I had never lifted anything heavier than a pencil for 14 years, I resolved to get out - anyhow work was very hard to arrive by in this poor old country.

It was a hard and sad wrench to leave my dear Rachel and those dear kids on that Friday evening at mother's home in Adolphus Street, Seaham when Uncle Jimmy and I set out for Liverpool. I remember well how it blew a strong gale during the overnight train journey.

We arrived in Liverpool in the early morning to see on the news boards about the Fleetwood fishing fleet being lost in the gale.

ABOARD THE SAMARIA BOUND FOR NEW YORK

The Cunard ship blew her horn at 10 a.m. when I waved a farewell goodbye to Uncle Jimmy (his brother) and we were on the waters. I had many mixed feelings and thoughts but like Sir Galahad's quote, "I have the strength of ten because my heart is pure." (It came back pure). It wasn't many hours before we were all scanning our eyes to see the last bit of England fade away and the passengers turned away from the ship's side, with different expressions of seeing the Homeland fade away, and nothing but sea, sea and sea all around. Everyone disappeared, myself included to get acquainted with their berths and the new life aboard the ship.

I shared a cabin with a chap from one of the Hetton collieries, Norman Jamison, a chap 6 foot 2 inches in height, he had been a machine gunner in the 1914 war. Despite the fact he was teetotal, I enjoyed his company during the trip, having our morning exercise on deck and sparring in the gym. He was too tall for me and I couldn't reach him, but he said I was fast.

We corresponded for many months after our arrival. He went to a sister in Boston. I have many times tried to find out about him but without success. Our morning exercise around the deck was short-lived for after 3 days at sea, it blew up a gale and everyone battened down below. I must say scouting around I found an open outlet to the deck and enjoyed that thrilling experience of watching those great Atlantic rollers smothering the ship. It was fascinating to watch, owing to having been battened down for so many days.

It was very hot and depressing not being able to get on deck. Many people were seasick all the time, one chap went mad and had to be locked up in his cabin. We sailed on a Saturday morning and did not arrive until the Tuesday week, many days overdue owing to the weather for these ships were almost new and twin screw 17 knots ships and weather permitting could do the journey from Liverpool to New York in six days.

Later when we arrived, everyone was glad to get onto dry land and get off that rolling, pitching ship!

I soon found the bar and spent some time in it, as there was nothing else to do or go. The opening hours were the same as ashore. It was quite a large panelled place, very comfortable,

only due to the ship's rolling, the panels moved and creaked with every roll which was inclined to get on one's nerves! I must say, I was never sick, and I never missed a meal - sometimes I was the only one at my table of 6 and really enjoyed it all!
We could buy a little Atlantic Daily Mail and see all the news of home.

ON TO ST. LOUIS TO MEET COUSIN BILL

After a weary buffeting trip we arrived in New York at 1:00 PM on a Tuesday and spent the next few hours going through customs and having dinner at a hotel. The "Cooksman" looked after everything - train tickets etc. He put our little party, some 40 of us who were going to St. Louis Illinois on the train at 6 p.m. It was a long journey some 1200 miles. We arrived at 7 a.m. on a Thursday morning. The carriages were very large. You could walk the full length of the train in comfort, sit out on the observation platform and enjoy the passing scenery. What a vast country it is!

I finally arrived at my destination, a small town called Edwardsville, a poor sort of town with nothing but wooden shacks for homes. There was no one at the station to meet me owing to the ship being overdue. My cousin Bill Jubb did not know when I would arrive.

The chap at the station somehow got in touch with him and Bill came down. He had no car so we walked back to his home. He then gave me the sad news that he had been laid off from his job and there was much unemployment around the district.

He said it all happened while I was on the way over. It wasn't a very good start for me! We spent the day and way into the night talking and talking and planning for both of us to find work. I had a few pounds left which soon fled away as Bill and I visited St. Louis and other places, but to no avail. Bill was the first to land a job. He came in one day and tossed a gun on the table. It had belonged to a crossing minder who had been shot. Bill had got his job. These were prohibition days when everyone packed a gun. I thought to myself, "What a country have I come to!"

PENNILESS AND JOBLESS

Here I was, left on my own with money run out and no work. However, I was very fit and confident despite the circumstances so I resorted to bumming right out of town to look for a job.

I met a bootlegger who went out of town each day. He and I got very matey. He dropped me off each day at a different town while I combed the place and then he picked me up at the spot he dropped me down.

After about a couple of weeks of this, I finally landed a job in a small town called Alton.

THE LARGEST BOTTLE WORKS IN THE U.S.

"What a job!", but I was desperate now and glad to tackle anything. It was all night shift seven days a week from 6:00 pm to 6:00 am with a half an hour break for lunch. It was at the largest bottle works in the US.

You couldn't get full board lodgings in this place so you had to eat all meals at the works canteen, thus life was just bed and work. The work was very heavy but interesting, filling up the moulds of every size and shape.

I stuck it out for about a week when I received a letter from the Labour supervisor of a place I had previously visited. This supervisor had been to Europe and England studying the working conditions so he remembered me when he offered me this job. It was an explosive factory but quite a tip-top place. I had fancied it when I had previously visited so I clinched the job right away.

THE WESTERN CARTRIDGE COMPANY EAST ALTON AND ADVENTURES WITH BEN KAY

The work was skilled and varied and very interesting. Away from what I had been used to, it was an all-day shift 7:30 am to 5:00 pm and one hour for lunch.

It was a very dangerous place. Almost every week there were explosions which killed or injured men. Hundreds of cars would rush down to the works to see if "their man" was okay. I wasn't many days at this place when a chap came along and introduced himself. His name was Ben Kay.

He had been in the US for five years with his wife and two children. They had a nice little home not far from the works (The Western Cartridge Company East Alton Illinois). He and I were the only Englishmen in the factory of some 5000 employees.

I visited his home very frequently which was a great help in such a lonely life in this vast country. They had a car - a Chevrolet and with him, his wife and his two children, we used to have many weekend tours around the country. He and I used to travel 40 miles to Saint Louis for a drink where he had some relations.

One early Sunday morning about 2 am, we were returning to his home. On coming over the Saint Louis bridge, suddenly there was a crash bang wallop as a big truck came tearing towards us with police sirens screaming behind them.

Ben moved quickly and saved a head-on collision, but the big truck wiped off our mudguards and pushed us over to the rails. I will never forget that moment when I was looking over into the Mississippi below. After we had collected ourselves together, we got on the road again. A few miles ahead, Ben spotted a roadhouse so we pulled in for a coffee.

We were both pretty shocked as we talked over the past accident on the bridge when a chap came around and said to me, "What part of England do you come from, Sunderland County Durham?" I said, "Well not far from there, a little place called Seaham Harbour."

He said, "Hello you do put it there boy! I come from Murton. My name is Anderson." He had been listening to our conversation about the accident. "I guess you two guys could do with a shot of whiskey. Follow me." We went underground to "Speak Easy" which had drinks of every kind - 50 Cent for about a tablespoon of whiskey! These were prohibition days. This chap and I had a real old chinwag about Seaham, Murton and all around the northeast coast.

He had been out in the USA for 15 years and was a naturalised Yank.

I wasn't with Ben Kay very long before he put me into the picture of just where I had landed in this factory. They just hated all English men for none of them had been overseas in the 1914 War to think and experience otherwise.

That area of the West States was isolationist and still is in 1964. The Klu Klux Klan were very strong and wielded much secret power. I soon found out that Ben's story of his experience there was only too true. I could fill a book 10 times this size with all the rotten tricks they used to do to try and get rid of you.

One Saturday morning, Ben did not turn up to work. I called at his home in the afternoon. He had sold his home with all his furniture, had his car packed and said he was off on safari. This was a blow to me for I had spent many happy hours with him and his family. I felt like the last lone man on a raft after his pal had gone over the side. I thought to myself, I am going to get out of this place with all its hatred of Englishman.

My first move was a long shot, I wrote to the editor of Buffalo Times requesting a monthly postal edition of his paper and telling him of how I wanted to work in Buffalo. By return came a bundle of papers which I scammed for about a couple of weeks when I spotted an ad for The Studebaker Car Corporation in South Bend which said, "If qualified and have tools, apply right away for an interview."

This job was about 400 miles north of St. Louis. I went down to the factory the next morning, all dressed up and told them I wanted to quit. They were okay with it. The supervisor who gave me the job was a Swede. He was the only guy in the place who liked Englishmen.

THE STUDEBAKER CAR CORPORATION SOUTH BEND INDIANA

Travelled overnight and arrived in South Bend on a lovely warm sunny Sunday morning.

This was in October 1928. I liked the town as soon as I entered it. There was music everywhere. Radios outside of shops were playing *Sonny Boy*, *There's a Rainbow round my shoulder* etc etc. Talkies were just coming out in the US.

I bought a local paper and searched for digs. A tall good-looking blonde came and said, "I guess you are looking for a room?" That was her job to hang around the station and spot people who might be interested in digs. I got into her car and she took me to a lovely home both inside and outside. It was 10 dollars a week. I soon found they wanted the dollars for the food was poor and scanty. The landlady was a widow. She ran a big Hudson car. She took me out for a drink once or twice. I could see she had designs on me so I quietly looked around for some other pastures which I soon found near the Studebaker factory at $7 a week.

A good grub house with other boarders whom I got on with very well. I was there about a couple of months when I fell out with the landlady's husband. He was German-born. He was always chipping away at me about England and royalty until I got fed up with him and that was the end of that joint. I next found a place right over on the outskirts of the city. They were smashing digs and a real top spot where I remained until I came home. They ran a Nash car and every weekend used to run me up to Lake Michigan and many other lovely places, for Indiana, is all flat country and very lovely. The man was very old and died while I was there. He was a retired butcher and just used to sit in the sun parlour all day. He had heart trouble and I used to sit with him for many hours. He liked to hear about England. Their daughter and son-in-law also lived with them. I was the only boarder and they treated me as one of the family. This was my fifth dig and I was really happy there.

However, I am running ahead of my story - to get back to Studebakers, I was down there on Monday morning and passed all the tests and questioning and started right away the next day. This place and all the people were the opposite of the last job for many of them had been overseas in the 1914 war and had actual experience of England and its people.

The bosses and the men were all ok. I remember one fellow

shouting out, "Hey boys, here's a Johnny Bull." There were many Johnny Bulls in this factory but they had been out from 10 to 40 years in the States. I was quite happy at this job and worked in many departments. It was a large factory-like town with teaming thousands. I had many friends who invited me to their homes. Almost every home in those prohibition days brewed their own beer, wines and whiskey. The latter was strong stuff. I couldn't bear the smell of it. There was squirrel whiskey which made you want to climb trees and mule whiskey that made you kick like a mule.

I stuck to the bottled beer. It wasn't very good but any port in a storm! I remember when the old gent died at this last digs, his widow said to me, "Saunders, would you like to drink that beer down in the basement?" They were around 100 bottles down there. I used to go down and polish off a few every so often for both her and her son-in-law did not drink.

This was now the summer of 1929 which had lovely, consistent hot weather which now and again became a heatwave, running up to 98 or 100 degrees but they never lasted very long, perhaps a couple of days. I enjoyed many weekends with the family around the shores of Lake Michigan, but as this summer was drawing out I could see conditions were getting thin in the USA. Unemployment was beginning to be talked about in the home and pressmen were being paid off each week at Studebakers. America had overproduced itself.

AMERICA HAD OVERPRODUCED ITSELF
Studebaker's had 27,000 cars in stock. The Great Wall Street crash, which came overnight at the end of 1929 was on its way! I decided that I would come home for, if you had no work, you

were on the rocks in the United States at that time.

Some two or three months before I did finally leave, Rachel told me there was no work in England. She sent a cable to this effect which stayed my hand, but I could see it was only a matter of time before I would be paid off.

Conditions were getting bad in all places (in the 1930s the US had 10,000,000 out of work), so in July 1929 I packed my bags and left a lovely job and the city of South Bend. I had spent nine happy months there. My boss took me up to the VIPs office and told them I was going back to England. One of them said, "If you ever come back to the States look us up. We'll give you a job." I could sense that they knew that the writing was on the wall.

When the crash did come in November 1929, many millionaires committed suicide. Erskine Studebaker did. I left with many happy memories of my time with them - just the opposite to my previous job in Illinois.

HOME ON THE LACONIA

Even today in March 1964 I don't know whether I would have transported my dear wife Rachel and children out there even if there hadn't been a crash, for it is a tough and fast country to live in.

At 40 years of age, I was really too old for that country, to take a young family out and dig a future for them. I did not come back a millionaire but at least I kept them going in those bad years of unemployment in England. I was always homesick deep down and longing for the day to see them all again.

When I was walking up the gangway to board the Laconia on that sunny day on July the 27th 1929, I was the happiest man in the US, home to England, to my wife and family. Only those who experienced this can understand the feeling! The voyage home was the opposite to the voyage out. The ship was delayed by a breakdown and we were overdue in Liverpool so Rachel had to stay at a hotel until I arrived. I ran along that quay and nearly crushed her to death. I wasn't long home before I landed a job in Billingham despite the unemployment.

We also moved up to Deneside in Seaham, to a lovely new house. Rachel should have moved out of the dump in Viceroy Street while I was away anyway. The Lord was good to all of us during that near 2-year absence. I have worked hard and prayed hard all my life for my dear wife and family. I have just passed my 77 years and am quite prepared to go to my loved ones. The Lord's will be done.

Also in 1964 Ernest wrote to his daughter Gladys and finished by giving her these verses from the Bible-

The Lord bless you and keep you: The Lord make his face shine upon you, and be gracious unto you: The Lord lift up his countenance upon you, and give you peace. Numbers 6:24-26

Less than three years after writing these memoirs, my grandfather Ernest departed this earth in 1967 aged 80.

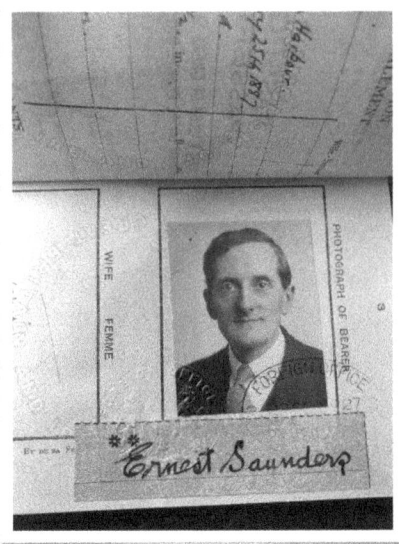

ERNEST'S PASSPORT PHOTO AGED 40.

FITTER'S HOUSE WHERE ERNEST STAYED IN CHICAGO.

6

THE HUGUENOTS

As I sift through old family photos, I find one of particular interest. It is a copy – so I have been told, of one of the earliest photos ever taken with the original being on a glass negative. The subject of this photo is from one of my father's family lines on his father's side. The story begins many centuries ago in the late 1300s when the De Henzell (sometimes called Henezel) family left their native Bohemia and settled in Alsace Lorraine.

Alsace and Lorraine were separated by the Vosges mountains. Alsace, after a stormy history marked by many mediaeval wars became definitely part of France in the 17th century during the reign of Louis XIV while Lorraine had been French in language and spirit since the 12th century.

The De Henzells lived in the Lorraine region and were Huguenots or protestants, and in predominantly Catholic France were much persecuted. French protestants preferred to be called "L'Eglise Reformee". The name Huguenot was originally a derogatory term from their opponents or accusers for "Les guenons de Hus" meaning "monkeys of Hus." Hus was martyred as a so-called heretic in the 1300s.

JOHN HUSS

John Huss came from the De Henzell family's native Bohemia and was born in the town of Hussenitz in 1372. John studied theology at the University of Prague and was ordained a priest and later made rector of the university. He and others in Bohemia were greatly influenced by the writings of John Wycliffe who was born in England in 1328 and died in 1384.

Wycliffe was known especially for his rejection of any biblical basis for a pope having absolute authority over the church, his insistence that the scriptures were the foremost authority in all church matters and his insistence on extensive reforms in the wealth, corruption and abuses of the Roman church. He believed that people should have a Bible in their own language so that they could read it for themselves (if they were literate), as all Bibles were in Latin and only used by the clergy and even sometimes chained to pulpits so they could not be removed.

The spread of these views in Bohemia was helped by the fact that a man known as Jerome of Prague had translated Wycliffe's writings from English into Czech. John Huss not only believed what Wycliffe wrote but he began teaching the views from his own pulpit.

The hierarchy of the church was certainly very corrupt during Huss's lifetime. At one time there were three competing popes. Despite support from university leaders, certain noble people - King Winceslaus and his wife- and being guaranteed safe conduct by Holy Roman Emperor Sigismund, when Huss was attending the Council of Constance, he was arrested and charged with heresy.

Unfortunately, Emperor Sigismund let Huss down and refused to intervene. This led to the Hussite wars after Huss's martyrdom as the Czech people regarded this as a national affront.

It was from this time and against this background that some members of the De Henzell family left their native Bohemia to settle in Lorraine.

In Desbois's Dictionary of the Nobles of France, published in 1770 the De Henzell family are mentioned as – originally a noble Bohemian family, the principal branch settled in Lorraine about four centuries prior to the publication of Desbois's Dictionary. Desbois's introductory notice of the "De Hennezel" (alternative spelling of De Henzell) family is as follows-
"Noblesse originaire du Royaume de Boheme, dont la principale est establie en Lorraine depuis environs quatre siecles." (Taken from website Geneanet by Phillip Adenbrooke)
The first Henzell recorded in Desbois's Dictionary is Henri Hennezel who married Isabeau d'Esche on May 30th 1392. He was maitre d'hotel to Charles, Duke of Lorraine.

THE FRENCH PERSECUTION OF THE HUGUENOTS
It was from about the mid-16th century that Protestants in France were called Huguenots. For 250 years they suffered persecution, France being a Roman Catholic country. In the year 1535, French king Francis 1st ordered that they should be killed. Despite being persecuted, more and more people joined them including some very important people but by 1562 it was very obvious to Edward De Henzell that he and his family needed to leave the country. As we can see from the description in Debois's Dictionary, branches of the Henzell family stayed in Lorraine as they were there in the 1770s.

THE HENZELLS LEAVE LORRAINE
Edward De Henzell looked up at the night sky and sighed. "Oh God," he prayed, "Will this persecution never end? Will we ever be free to worship you in this country?" He loved the district of Alsace Lorraine where many generations of his family had lived.

It was at this point that he decided that at least for the time being, he, his family and friends needed to leave. He talked of this plan to the others and they all agreed and so it was that the De Henzells and their relatives the Tyzacs (original surname Du Thisac) and others with them set off for England.

England was now protestant, as Elizabeth 1st had come to the throne after the reign of her half-sister, Mary. Mary was called Bloody Mary because, in her attempt to re-establish the Roman Catholic religion, she caused many people to be martyred.

Edward, his family and friends chose to settle in Newcastle-upon-upon-Tyne in the North East of England. They landed at St. Peter Quay Wallsend in Newcastle and brought their skills in glass making. (Elizabeth reigned from 1558 to 1603) and in 1568, the De Henzells, or the Henzells as they later became called were engaged to manufacture glass in Newcastle.

In later centuries, there are Henzells engaged in shipbuilding in Seaham Harbour and their relatives, the Tyzacks are recorded as having an ironworks company in the Monkwearmouth district of Sunderland in the 1800s.

THE ST. BARTHOLOMEW'S DAY MASSACRE

Their departure was very timely as it was only around four years later that the horrific massacre of the Huguenots began on St Bartholomew's Day August the 24th 1572. It originated in Paris and spread throughout France for two months until 100,000 protestants were killed and the Huguenots were nearly extinguished from the face of the Earth. (However even with these Huguenots gone, by 1661 Protestants numbered about 1 million).

People were tortured and killed in horrific ways. In the first 3 days, nearly 10,000 bodies were counted in Paris alone. They threw the bodies into the Seine river until the water was red as blood. The butchery was so continuous that along the street gutters in Paris, blood ran like water after a rainstorm.

Women were raped and murdered and their children were disembowelled. A writer at that time called Foxe described everything in different districts of France in detail in his book, *Foxes Book of Martyrs*. Although the Henzell and Tyzack families in Newcastle must have been relieved that they had escaped before this massacre occurred, how heartbroken they must have felt. There undoubtedly must have been people in Lorraine whom they knew, who had been murdered.

The man who first carried the news of the massacre to Rome was rewarded by being given 1000 crowns by the Cardinal of Lorraine. In the later 1600s, more than 400,000 Huguenots fled from France, many to England following more persecution, which was France's loss, as they were a hard-working people with many skilled craftsmen, as were the Henzells and Tyzacks with their glass-making skills.

Isabella Henzell was descended from these families. Her father, John Henzell was a glassmaker and she married John Capstaff who was born in Amsterdam and was also a glassmaker. Their daughter Mary was my paternal grandfather's father's grandmother. Mary was born in Newcastle in 1809 and died aged 49 in 1858 leaving some quite young children. In the 1861 census, her eldest daughter, Margaret (my grandfather's grandmother) had her younger sister, Susannah living with her including her son, my grandfather's father, John Booth Richardson aged three.

Mary is in the photo with a young boy. Mary married Hamlet Booth at St. Andrew's Church Newcastle in 1830. Hamlet was born in Yorkshire in 1811 and was a potter. In those early days of photography, the subject had to keep very still for a long time which probably accounts for the miserable expressions on both their faces as Mary had to make sure that her young charge kept still! As mentioned earlier, I have been told that this is one of the earliest photographs ever taken and is on a glass negative. The 1851 census has Mary with her children, lodging with another family. Hamlet is not there so this must have been the time when according to family members, he went to work with potters in Spain.

I am not sure why John Capstaff, Mary's father was born in Amsterdam, but my father's younger brother, Uncle Malcolm remembers that during his childhood, his father, went on a visit to Amsterdam and later wondered if it was to visit relatives, as not many people travelled outside the U.K at that time as it was rather expensive.

Mary Booth nee Capstaff with a young boy

7

GEORGE AND MARY

My paternal grandfather George Henry Winship Richardson was born on the 18th of April 1892 at 10 Mount Pleasant, Sunderland to John Booth Richardson (born Durham 1857) whose occupation was a ship's plater and Margaret Richardson nee Winship (born Burnmoor 1860.) They were married in St. Barnabas Church, Burnmoor, Durham when John was 25 and Margaret 22.

John and Margaret went on to have six children of which George was the youngest. There was Margaret the oldest who was 10 years older than George and four older brothers between her and George.

His older brothers were Joseph born in 1883, Charles born in 1885, John born in 1887 and Francis born in 1890. Unfortunately, George never knew his father who died when he was still a baby in 1893. His mother subsequently remarried to John Baty and had two more girls, Dora four years younger than George and later Muriel.

GEORGE'S GRANDPARENTS

As already mentioned at the end of the last chapter, George's paternal grandmother was Margaret Richardson nee Booth (born in Newcastle in 1832.)

Margaret was the daughter of Mary Booth nee Capstaff seen in the photo in the previous chapter. (Mary married Hamlet Booth on December 12th 1830. He was a potter and was born in

Yorkshire). George's paternal grandfather Charles Richardson (born 1830 in Heworth, a district of Newcastle-upon-Tyne) whose profession was an Iron Shipwright married Margaret Booth (born 1833) in Newcastle in 1854.

George's maternal grandparents were Joseph Winship who was born in Penshaw Durham in 1826 and Frances Ramshaw born in Lumley Durham in 1831. Joseph was a miner. They were married in 1850.

George married my grandmother, Mary Ann Merchant on June 12th 1916 when he was 24 years old and Mary was 22. His family home at the time was 234 Chester Road, Sunderland and Mary's was 79 St. Leonard's Street, Sunderland.

According to my father, his main interests were gardening, running and sport in general. I understand that he won cups for his running and also for bowling in later life.

EARLIEST, RATHER INDISTINCT PHOTO OF GEORGE

MEMORIES OF GRANDPA RICHARDSON

Grandpa Richardson always seemed a rather proper man. I was a little bit in awe of him. My grandmother seemed to fill the house with him being more in the background. Looking back, I just think that he wasn't at ease relating to children but when he came to live with us for a while during my teenage years, I got to know him better and appreciated how loving and caring he was.

He was very tall at six foot, for a man born in the 1890s and a very good sportsman, particularly running and in his older years he played bowls for the county. He was a good musician and was at one time a church organist. One of his favourite hymns was "The day Thou gavest Lord has ended," which was actually a relatively modern hymn for him, the author having only just died before Grandpa was born.

I particularly remember when he and my grandmother were living in Leominster Road Sunderland, they had a house on a corner plot that he made into a beautiful garden. Grandpa Richardson lived into his 90s.

Grandpa Richardson was not a man to waste words or "beat around the bush" as the old saying goes. I have a rare letter which he wrote to my father during the second World War. He usually left letter writing to my grandmother. It is interesting that he only mentions business matters concerning the car insurance, (which was for a Morris Saloon, horse power 10 and registration GR 3990) the weather and my father's problems with his leg and says that is all the news. If my grandmother had been writing she would have probably mentioned family members and maybe friends.

29 Woodville Cres. Sunderland May 1943

Dear George,

Received your letter through your Mother and was pleased you arrived back to Newark OK. I passed Newark on Thurs.6th @ 12/5 coming back from London. I thought of you, when the train rattled through the stations (non stop). How did the car answer the call, when going down? Enclosed find cover note for car. Mr. Ducker is attending to the insurance & hope to receive the certificate in due course. I will let you know when I receive same.
Now George, how is your leg? Have you seen the doctor yet? Don't forget to let me know the report & look after same. We had a terrible day yesterday (Monday) it was snowing all day & the ground is covered about 2ins. thick. When I came out to work this morning the fields in front of our house were a mantle of snow. Today it is fine & the sun shining, it is going away fast. Well, George this is all the news. So cheerio & take care of yourself

With love, Dad

GEORGE HENRY WINSHIP ON HIS RETIREMENT

NANNA RICHARDSON

Mary Ann (nee Merchant) Richardson.

Mary was born at 28 Frances Street, Seaham Harbour on June 30th 1895 to George Henry (born Seaham Harbour 1871 and died Sunderland 1937) who was a mineral water manufacturer and Jane Ann (nee Armstrong) Merchant (born Seaham Harbour 1871 and died Sunderland 1948). Her sister, Annie Ellen and only sibling, was born the next year on July 27th 1896. They were a very close-knit family.

MARY'S GRANDPARENTS

Mary's maternal grandfather, Francis Lewins Armstrong, a blacksmith by trade was born in Seaham Harbour in 1852 and married Mary Ann Cutty who was born in Quarrington Hill, Durham in 1851. The Armstrong branch of the family can be traced to Cresswell on the north Northumberland coast.

Mary's paternal grandfather, William Merchant (christened December 1827 in Christchurch Tynemouth) was a mariner and later a dock pilot. He was born in North Shields Northumberland in 1827 and his wife Ellen nee Deacon, Mary's grandmother was born in Grinton, Yorkshire in 1829. We can see that Mary Ann and her sister, Annie Ellen were probably named after their grandmothers!

MEMORIES OF NANNA RICHARDSON

Mary Ann, my grandmother, was one of the kindest persons I have ever encountered. My grandfather, being the head buyer for the House of Fraser men's department store in Sunderland called Binns, was able to get a 25% discount on purchases.

She made full use of this with my grandfather apparently not always being pleased, according to my father. Much of what she bought were things for others. My father told me that she bought a new washing machine because there were some problems with the old one but when she encountered a needy mother with quite a large family who didn't have a washing machine, Mary gave her the new one which she had just purchased. George was not impressed!

She was very maternal and family orientated. As a child, I knew she deeply loved us all. According to my uncle Malcolm her youngest son, she was pregnant eleven times and lost eight babies in order to have her three boys so that probably made them all the more precious to her.

This accounted for the large gaps in their ages. She was fortunate to have her mother and sister living nearby, and both my father and his youngest brother Malcolm told me that it was like having three mothers, especially as Annie Ellen (or Auntie Nellie as we called her) married too late to have her own children.

My first memories of my grandmother Mary was of her bouncing me up and down on her knee and singing a song which went something like this –

Oh my Mary Ann, when she got up at the top, her heart went flipperty flop. The wheel began to stop. The man in the moon looked down too soon and Mary began to cry. She lost her situation through the great big wheel!

The song started off slowly and then speeded up and when she reached the line, "She lost her situation through the great big wheel" she would open her legs so that I would fall to the ground and giggle. This invariably brought cries of, "Again! Again!" from me!

My parents and sister went to live down south when my mother was pregnant with me. One Christmas during my childhood, we didn't go up to Sunderland so our grandmother sent presents to us. Unfortunately, we rather rudely forgot to send a thank you note. My grandfather told my father that it made her cry. It is only as many years have gone by that I have realised how much she must have missed having our family nearby, particularly with my sister and I being her only grandchildren at that time.

LEFT TO RIGHT – Jean Brunskill (who married Roy, their second son) George, Mary and youngest son, Malcolm.

8

ERNEST AND RACHEL

There is already quite a lot of information in this book about my maternal grandfather, Ernest, written in his own hand. As mentioned earlier, he was the son of Charles Saunders and Isabella Saunders nee Gray (born Stockton 1862), his paternal grandparents being Captain James Saunders and Dorothy Saunders nee Wylam. Ernest, with his siblings and parents are shown in the photo at the end of chapter 3.

His maternal grandparents were James Gray and Elizabeth Gray nee Baird. James was a bottle maker and was born in South Shields in 1836. Elizabeth was also born in South Shields in 1839. The family had settled in Seaham Harbour by the time Isabella's younger brother was born in 1860. By the time of the 1901 census, when my grandfather was aged 14, his grandfather, James Gray aged 65 was a widower and living with his daughter Isabella and the family.

MEMORIES OF GRANDPA SAUNDERS - ERNEST

I had a special bond with Grandpa Saunders and I knew that he would do almost anything for me. I was the youngest of all his grandchildren, some of whom were almost old enough to be my parents. I remember that he loved history and English literature. He was an avid reader and would write a review of each book he read in the back of his diary. I always loved visiting him because he was a great talker and sometimes quite funny.

I particularly remember one occasion when I went with him to visit Uncle Sid, his eldest son, in Seaham. The weather was not good and it has been snowing. The bus didn't arrive and so I persuaded him to walk all the way to Seaham several miles away. He must have been around 74 or 75 years old which seemed old for those days as life expectancy was not as good as it today.

Often when I saw him he would give me a hug and lift me off the ground. The last time he did this was when I was twelve and had nearly reached my adult height of 5ft 6 inches. He, himself was only 5ft 8 inches. He seemed very pleased with himself that he could still do it.

Some years later, after his wife Rachel, my grandmother died, after completing my course in London I planned to go and live with him, as I was concerned that he might be feeling lonely. However, it was not to be, as he died the year before I could get there.

NANNA SAUNDERS NEE BARKER

Rachel was born in Seaham Harbour in 1889 at 28 Cornish Street. She married my grandfather in 1911 when she was 22. She was living at 35 Adolphus Street West at the time with my grandfather's family, her mother having died when Rachel was in her teens. Rachel was the daughter of Robert Barker (born in Seaham Harbour in 1850) who was a blacksmith and Elizabeth Robinson (born in Broomeside Durham in 1856 and died at 28 Cornish Street, Seaham Harbour on 12th May 1907). Her parents were married in Christchurch, Seaham Harbour in 1871 when Elizabeth was only fifteen.

Rachel was one of nine children. There was Hannah born 1873, Mary Ann born 1875, Thomas born 1876, George born 1877, Jane born 1882, Elizabeth born 1884, Mathew born 1895 and Margaret born 1897.

Rachel's mother, Elizabeth died in 1907 and her father, Robert married again the following year to Sarah born in 1850. Elizabeth's family are recorded in the 1861 census. Her mother, Rachel's maternal grandmother, Hannah (nee Charlton born in Harelow Durham 1819) had been recently widowed and left with seven children (including Elizabeth only 3 years old) and her youngest – baby Hannah, was only five months old. She had married Thomas, her deceased husband at St. Lawrence Church Pittington on 7th March 1840) Her husband, Thomas (Rachel's maternal grandfather) had been a coal miner. He was born in Houghton-le-Spring in 1817 and died in Seaham Harbour on 10th May 1860. Both Thomas and Hannah came from mining families. Hannah's father, Mathew had been a miner as had Thomas's father also called Thomas.

The family were living at 38 California Row, Seaton Colliery, Seaham. The three eldest boys are listed as being coal miners. Matthew is just sixteen years old, Thomas only thirteen most shocking of all, is William aged only ten.

On the 7th of May 1842, MPs read a report by a royal commission on conditions of employment of children in industries such as the mines. This report was illustrated by drawings on the spot and showed the cruelty exacted upon these children in mines owned by the so-called nobility of England. There were girls chained to heavy carts drawing coals up low, narrow passages, far underground. They were sometimes sexually abused.

Children of five or even younger were working trap doors without light in rat-infested mines. Children were standing all day ankle-deep in water at the pumps for 12 to 16 hours a day and sometimes children were kept underground night and day. Some of the overseers were brutal and used a strap or even pick handles continually to punish or oppress them.

One lady reported that her boy aged ten had his toe cut off by a blind falling, but the loader made him work until the end of the day despite the fact that he was in great pain.

There were children on all fours who dragged and pushed the heavy sleds of coal. There were mines which had seams so low that they could only be worked by a small naked boy lying on his back with a little pick. These boys nearly all grew up deformed. Children climbed ladders with baskets of coals on their backs secured with straps around their heads and they were often punished or abused by the men.

Parliament abolished the slavery of women and children in the mines in the 1840s yet here is ten-year-old William still working in a mine in the 1860s. However, these were hard times to be without work or means of support. The awful prospect of the workhouses were the only alternative if you were destitute. These were often overcrowded places with hard labour in return for meagre food, disease was rife and the death rate high. They did not formally end until 1930 but there were still some functioning until 1948 when the National Assistance Act was passed.

Nanna Saunders' paternal grandfather was George Barker born 1824 in Seaham Harbour and died 1904. (His father was Robert Barker from Monkwearmouth, Sunderland). George was a master blacksmith and his wife, Hannah, nee Whittington, Nanna Saunders' grandmother was born 1826 in Shadforth, Durham. George and Hannah were married on the 8th of May 1847 Their family are recorded as living at 23 Australia Row, Seaton Colliery Seaham in the 1861 census.

(In the 1841 census George Barker aged 17 is recorded as being an apprentice blacksmith and living with Joshua and Mary Paxton in Seaham Harbour).

MEMORIES OF NANNA SAUNDERS NEE BARKER

I remember Nanna Saunders being a rather quiet lady. My cousin Geoff who was raised in the North East also found her to be very quiet. She wasn't at all well during the time I knew her. She died when I was thirteen. I remember my parents saying that she was on too many pills which caused side effects. My grandfather looked after her really well. I did get the impression that she was a very kind lady as although they didn't appear well off in old age, she once gave me quite a lot of money which she had saved up in a large jar.

However, my sister, being older than me remembers her when she was well and has memories of how Nanna and our mother enjoyed going on regular trips to the cinema.

LADY ON THE LEFT IS BELIEVED TO BE RACHEL SAUNDERS NEE BARKER WITH SISTER-IN-LAW, DOROTHY SAUNDERS AND AN UNIDENTIFIED BABY.

ERNEST AND RACHEL IN THEIR LATTER YEARS.

9

GEORGE AND DEREEN

My mother Dereen was born to Ernest and Rachel Saunders in Seaham Harbour on Tuesday, November 11th 1919. She was christened Mabel Doreen Saunders but was always addressed by her second name, "Doreen" which was always pronounced "Dereen."

Dereen was the baby of the family. The sibling who was nearest in age to her was her sister Gladys who was more than five years older, being born in 1914 and her brothers Arthur and Sidney were born in 1913 and 1912 respectively.

The only grandparent I remember my mother speaking about was Isabella Saunders nee Gray (James and Dorothy's daughter-in-law). It was probable that she was the only grandparent she knew.

As mentioned earlier, Isabella was married to Charles Saunders Dereen's paternal grandfather (James and Dorothy's only son). I remember my mother speaking of her granny with great affection and I have a prayer book which her granny gave her when she was ten and also a battered old photograph of her with granny taken at the seaside with Dereen on a donkey.

Dereen's maternal grandparents, also mentioned earlier were Robert Barker (born Seaham Harbour 1850) who was a blacksmith and Elizabeth nee Robinson (born Broomeside, Durham 1856) They were married at Christchurch Seaham Harbour in 1871.

ARTHUR AND SIDNEY WITH THEIR AUNTIE.

**Dorothy (Bertie Saunders' daughter), Sidney and Gladys
with Dereen, the small child in front.**

RATHER FADED PHOTO OF DEREEN WITH HER GRANDMOTHER, ISABELLA SAUNDERS NEE GRAY.

GEORGE HENRY MERCHANT RICHARDSON

George Henry Merchant Richardson, my father was born in Sunderland on Sunday 28th of April 1918 to George Henry Winship Richardson and Mary Ann Richardson nee Merchant. I believe he was named after his father and maternal grandfather both of whom were George Henrys. The "Merchant" was his mother's maiden name. His paternal grandparents were John Booth Richardson and Margaret Richardson nee Winship and his maternal grandparents were George Henry Merchant and Jane Ann Merchant nee Armstrong all mentioned in chapter 7. George's adult height was 5ft 9 inches and he had dark brown hair and hazel eyes.

I know more about my father's early life than my mother's as I recorded some of it while helping look after him when he was dying, so much of the following is in his own words.

George was the eldest of three boys, his father George was 25 when he was born and his mother Mary Ann was 23. His brothers were Royston (or Roy) Winship, Winship being their paternal grandmother's maiden name. George said that Roy weighed 13 1/2 pounds at birth. He was born on the 23rd of December 1926 in Sunderland.

GEORGE AND ROY AS CHILDREN

George's youngest brother was Malcolm Colin who was born on the 7th of February 1933 in Sunderland. George said he weighed 11 1/2 lbs at birth. (Both rather large babies!) George got on well with both his brothers but said that he did occasionally fight with Roy. George said that he didn't recall much about his brothers growing up as there were big gaps between their ages and also the war years didn't help.

GEORGE AND ROY AS CHILDREN

HOME LIFE

George's childhood home was 29 Woodville Crescent in the Grindon area of Sunderland and he had the bedroom over the porch. He recalled that they had a maid to help his mother run the house. His father George did a lot of work in the garden. George said, "I had a very privileged childhood with lots of toys. We got 25% off anything we wanted from Binns where my father worked and my mother made full use of this. Sometimes there were arguments between my parents because of this!"

"My favourite toy was an electric train - the Caerphilly Express (the Caerphilly Express ran from London to the South West, I think). It was the envy of all my friends. However, my best birthday memory was when I received a bicycle as a present. My favourite sports were cricket and tennis. My favourite meal was roast beef and Yorkshire pudding and my least favourite being liver and kidneys."

"I was given pocket money. I can't remember the amount but I spent it on sweets. We had the usual Christmas traditions that are still the same today. Every new year we would have a tall dark haired friend of the family come round at midnight which we called "First footing"."

SCHOOL DAYS

"My first school which I started to attend at the age of about 4 was St. Anthony's Montessori School. Nuns taught us and Sister Mary Austin was the head. My lifelong friend Dougie Eades also went there. Later, I went to Cowen Terrace School. While I was there I remember being given a patch of garden to cultivate but I used to escape through a hole in the hedge and play football.

All my memories of school days are very pleasant. My senior school was the Bede Collegiate Grammar School. I always walked to school and my friend Dougie Eades was also with me throughout my school career. Jack Davison was another friend. We all wore blazers with very ornate badges. I really liked it there and never got into trouble. We had a lot of homework and I particularly remember the maths teacher who was terrific and also the English teacher. Maths was my favourite subject.

The only subject which I didn't like was French. I got on with most of the teachers except the French teacher! My father employed a private tutor for extra French lessons and I didn't get on with him either! He would tell me that there were rules in French but I couldn't cope with all the exceptions to the rules!"

"I was so pleased that on gaining my Oxford certificate they awarded me a compensatory pass in French as I did so well in maths."

"I learnt to play the piano and the violin. I did get into trouble with my piano teacher - he wasn't pleased when I memorised a piece of music and when asked where I was on the page of music, said I didn't know!"

"After leaving school I trained to become an inspector of weights and measures with the Weights and Measures department of Sunderland District Council, a job I really enjoyed. I travelled each weekday by tram to West Wear Street near the River Wear to get to work. My wages were given into a family pot and my mother gave me spending money. My generous grandmother Merchant bought me my first car when I was 19 which gave me greater freedom and I and my friends Dougie Eades and Jack Davison used to go on holiday together in the Lake District area." (This car could have well as been a Morris Saloon for which I have an insurance cover note which my grandfather sent to my father in 1943).

"During the years leading up to the war, I often had arguments with my parents about me coming home too late at night but all that changed when war was declared when I was 21 and I joined the RAF."

BEDE COLLEGIATE GRAMMAR SCHOOL ORCHESTRA. GEORGE WITH HIS VIOLIN ON THE EXTREME RIGHT 3RD ROW FROM THE FRONT.

GEORGE'S FIRST DRIVING LICENSE WAS ISSUED A MONTH AFTER HIS 18th BIRTHDAY IN 1936.

GEORGE MIDDLE OF BACK ROW AGED 19, AT A COUNCIL SUMMER SCHOOL

GEORGE IN FANCY DRESS.

GEORGE IN HIS RAF UNIFORM.

10

GEORGE AND DEREEN AND THE 2ND WORLD WAR

Dougie Eades was one of my father's lifelong friends and the following is an extract from a book he wrote about the 2nd World War in 1996. In the copy, he gave to my father, Dougie wrote, "For my old and dear friend, George." Dougie and his fianceé were on holiday with my parents when they heard the news that Britain was at war with Germany.

"In fine sunny weather, a little group of holidaymakers, including my fiancée usually known as Chic, had enjoyed a week of rambling in the Lake District. Not a spot of rain had fallen and we had been free to roam the lanes or scramble amongst the hills day after day, confident that the weather was set fair and that the blue skies would continue to provide the right conditions for an open-air life. At the start of our second week, the Sunday morning dawned peacefully with pockets of mist lying sleepily in the valleys between the hills overlooking Lake Windermere. The air was still, the sky clear and every promise of another fine day in Ambleside was in prospect. Unfortunately, the weather would have little effect on the events of the day.

In the Lake District

The date was the 3rd of September 1939 and the time was 11 a.m. All companions so full of happy chatter in the past week had grown silent as we gathered around the radio to listen to Prime Minister Chamberlain make his historic announcement in which he said that since the German Chancellor had ignored the ultimatum which had been issued earlier, our country was now at war with Germany.

The silence amongst us continued as the strains of the national anthem died away. It was the end of all the uncertainty which had existed for the previous 4 years or so during which time Hitler had ranted raved and threatened all those who opposed his actions and policies. His massive rearmament programme and his aggressive entry into Poland had been too much, the limit had been reached.

That war had come was for many of us a relief, but as I'm looking back, this seems a trifle odd since in fact, the uncertainty about an impending war had only been replaced by a greater uncertainty about what the future might hold. Germany had been preparing for years and was militarily very strong. Britain was relatively weak and therefore vulnerable. Dangerous times were obviously ahead for both civilians and service personnel.
Nevertheless except for a few misguided pacifists, the vast majority of the nation held the view that right was on our side and come what may, the war had to be fought. It was now up to the younger members of the community to follow in the footsteps of their fathers in the first world war and show what they could do. Although we still had a week of our holiday to go, we decided that in the circumstances, home was the better place to be.
We would start for Sunderland that afternoon. Meanwhile Chic and I took a last lingering look at the countryside by walking slowly up to a favourite spot of ours on the Kirkstone Pass where we could enjoy a glimpse of Lake Windermere and the Langdale Valley with its familiar and distinctive pikes. Our panoramic and peaceful view was shattered suddenly by the wail of air-raid warning sirens in Ambleside.
A small civilian aircraft flew over the pass shortly afterwards and we looked at each other questioningly – a precursor of things to come perhaps? It certainly was for both of us, but perhaps more so on my account, since the sound of sirens and the sight of an aircraft would become very much a part of my life in the years ahead.
It was with much regret later in the afternoon that along with our friends George and Dereen, we pointed our Morris 12

in the homeward direction by making for Kendal. Here we stopped for some refreshments and were astonished to hear that Tyneside some 7 miles to the north of Sunderland as the crow flies, had been bombed - all codswallop of course but an example as to how rumours can fly in wartime. We arrived home during the evening to find everyone fully convinced that air raids were imminent.

Logically, one could not dispute the fact that the northeast coastal towns of England were exposed and easy targets for any marauding enemy bombers. The night sky was clear and brilliantly moonlit - a positive bombers moon and Hitler would undoubtedly take swift revenge - or so it was thought. Our fears were of course groundless and although great events took place in France and the Low Countries in the following months, Wearside did not experience enemy action until June 1940.

George and I had been friends since childhood and had only just missed being called up in the militia some weeks earlier and now, at the age of 21, we would obviously be in the first group to be conscripted.

We decided that the light blue uniform of the Royal Air Force was much better than khaki and as neither of us had salt in our veins, the Navy held no attraction. We would therefore volunteer for the junior service at the first opportunity. The next day we made our way to the local recruiting office and presented to the recruitment sergeant who was very receptive. The wheels began to turn astonishingly quickly. Almost immediately we were sent for medical examination and having been pronounced fit found that the skids had been smartly placed under us. We were told to report that evening and in doing so were promptly put on a train bound for Bedford.

We travelled all night and arrived at RAF Cardington early the next morning. So, in less than 48 hours of being on holiday, we were sworn in as brand new aircraft men AC plonks. It was now the 5th of September and I was allocated to my new service number 93-52-53 and told that I would be trained as a balloon rig fabric worker. I suspect that Cardington, with its huge airship hangars where aircraft such as the R100 and the R101 were built and which later had become the chief balloon centre, was somewhat biased towards its own genealogy.

George was going to be trained as a pilot but since he had suffered a bout of enteritis some weeks previously he could not pass the searching medical test and was sent home for two months in order to regain hundred percent fitness. So we bade each other farewell at Cardington, little knowing that we would not meet again for three-and-a-half years and in circumstances that neither of us could ever have been able to forecast."

My father, George wrote that he "had sufficient academic qualifications which made it possible to go on the flying training course without having to sit the entrance examination and pilots were needed in a hurry."

It was 1943 before Dougie and my father, George met up again. I quote again from Dougie's book –

"Chic had written to say that our old friend George, whom I had last seen at Cardington on day 3 of the war, had trained as a pilot in Texas, USA, and was now stationed at RAF Swinderby, about 10 miles southwest of Lincoln. I rang him and we arranged to meet in two days' time provided "Butch" Harris did not claim priority.

George was now a flight Lieutenant and had married Dereen who was in the WAAFs and was joining him that week-end on leave. He had started his operational tour a few weeks later than ours, and with this, and what happened in the intervening years, there would obviously be a lot to talk about. However, to cut a long story short we met as arranged and having compared notes it turned out that we had both been on the Stettin and Spezia raids."

My father had travelled to Texas for an eleven-week pilot's course but ended up staying longer due to an appendectomy. He said that to get to Texas, they disembarked at Newfoundland and then had a six-day train trip. He said that Lord Mannering was on his course and while he was in Texas, he met Lord and Lady Halifax. Halfway through the course, the Japanese attacked Pearl Harbour."

The following three air raids were ones that both Dougie and my father took part in and are described in Dougie's book - *The Turrets of War*.

SPEZIA

"Spezia was on the west coast of northern Italy. More than 200 aircraft would take part, and nearly all Lancasters and Italian warships were known to be in the port. The force included seven cruisers amongst them were - *Gorizia, Bolzano and Taranto*, also a mixture of destroyers and torpedo boats.

We would carry 5 × 1,000lb bombs and a much-reduced load of 180 × 4lb and 16 × 30lb incendiary bombs and our instructions were to attack the ships if they could be seen. Spezia must be the best part of 1000 miles by the route to be taken – a long way from home should mechanical trouble develop or damage be sustained over or near the target.

Fortunately, the Eighth Army had been doing well in North

Africa and newly released airfields there were operational. If necessary we could divert to them, which was a comforting thought. The route over France was quiet and although we flew near Paris I could not pinpoint its position. The Germans had obviously imposed their blackout restrictions as thoroughly as they had done in their own country but, in addition, they made sure that the Parisians complied - not an easy task.

Eventually, we turned south-east over southern France and headed towards the mountains. The snow-covered Alps by moonlight are a sight not to be forgotten and interest was supplied, presumably, by members of the Maquis who let their presence be known by flashing lights and lighting fires here and there in the mountains and valleys as we flew over them.

However, in the middle of this magnificent scenery I was enjoying, suddenly, nearly the whole turret was coated with a layer of ice. I reported this to the skipper who to my surprise did not seem too perturbed. As the Bay of Genoa loomed up, I changed position forward to the astrodome and maintained observation from there during the more dangerous period over the target. (Astrodome – a transparent observation dome on top of the fuselage used normally by navigators when taking astroshots.)

We were to bomb at 9000 feet - a much lower level than normal - consequently much more ground detail could be seen despite the fact that a smokes screen was operating to the north of the town and was drifting across the aiming point in the north-west wind. The fleet could not be seen and there was no alternative other than to bomb the port installations and town which could be more readily identified. Tommy was satisfied with his bombing run and, with the bombs gone, we set course for home.

Many bomb bursts were seen around the point of aim where fires started and rapidly gained a firm hold. A number of large explosions were observed in the same area during the attack, followed by others which were seen some twenty minutes after leaving the target. It is believed that heavy damage had been sustained by the dock area in Spezia."

SECOND SPEZIA OPERATION
"This time a smaller Force took part - less than 200 - and the same bomb load was carried. The moon has risen and we proceeded over France in quiet conditions, so much so that I can't, in fact, recall seeing any searchlights or flak north of Genoa. As an aid to navigation the Pathfinders were supposed to drop landmark flares over Lac du Bourget. (Aix-les-Bains). We saw the flares but no lake and could only assume that they had been dropped slightly out of position. The weather was clear, the moon was high and a snow covered ridges of the Alps ahead promised another scenic treat. As we rose over the peaks other Lancasters appeared and we flew together for a while through superb mountain vistas before slowly diverging due possibly to small navigation adjustments to course. The visibility conditions were extraordinary, at least 50 miles, I would judge, and possibly twice that distance but I failed to identify Mont Blanc, although it must have been visible. Eventually as we descended gradually to a bomb height of 8000 feet over the Bay of Genoa, the shoreline stood out clearly, dividing the plush coppice land mass from the luminous serenely calm sea. The whole scene was one of peaceful tranquility.

On approach to Spezia uncoordinated searchlights began crazy merry-go-round movements and some Italian gunners were hosepiping light flak all over the sky quite ineffectively. It was easy to imagine defending crews gesticulating and shouting excitedly at one another and generally running about in all directions like headless chickens. Their performance was the antipathy of the cool, efficient, ruthless approach of the Germans which we respected.

However, the smokescreen was better this time and made the bomb aimer's job more difficult. Nevertheless, with the aid of red ground markers Tommy dropped his bombs and off we went. The raid was perhaps not so effective as on the previous occasion but was judged to have been concentrated and generally successful.

On the way home we noticed a respectable and steady searchlight cone over Turin the likes of which they did not even attempt at Spezia. If this was one of our chaps someone was really off course. How this could happen in such perfect flying conditions is beyond comprehension but a more likely explanation is that the local searchlight unit was just having a quiet training session to themselves.

Our return journey was quiet and without incident. We had been routed to fly over central London on our way back home for morale purposes, though I'm not sure that all Londoners would appreciate a force of heavy bombers thundering over at 2000 feet so early in the morning. However, our presence had been picked up by the BBC and the announcer who, after greeting us, mentioned to the world that the boys of Bomber Command were returning from a raid. He then played the RAF March in our honour."

STETTIN

"The uncovered map revealed a track ribbon leading up over the North Sea, turning over Denmark and across the length of the Baltic Sea to Stettin. The best was yet to come. Wing commander Woods stood up, paused, gazed around the crews over his "half eyes" and with an impish smile, announced that we were to fly low-level both ways below radar detection height. Near pandemonium broke out... Crumbs!

Flying at zero feet to a target 600 miles away... We were all excited except Joe who, I think, was trying to weigh up what navigational problems might ensue... Whatever, it was going to be quite a night. The weather was set fair, the night cloudless and moonlit and this would be in our favour. The bombing run would be made after a climb to 10,000 feet near the target. The bomb load was a cookie and the usual mixture of incendiary bombs.

About 340 aircraft would take part but only Group 1 Lancasters would be flying low level... Groups 3 and 5 had the option of flying at a low level or at 12,000 feet. It was still light when we set off... Maurice was in his element as we hedge-hopped over the countryside and we sped along just missing this or that obstruction in a way only he could.

The Lincolnshire coastline loomed ahead and the seals, always in great numbers around The Wash - must have dived for cover as we sped over the North Sea skimming the waves in the brilliantly clear weather. It was a long stretch over the sea to Denmark and there was much time to contemplate the "joys" of ditching if anything should go wrong... God, there wouldn't be much time to act if anything happened and most likely we would just disappear into a cloud of spray... A clean sweep one might say. Such thoughts had to be firmly put to the back of one's mind.

Eventually, the coast of Denmark came into view – landfall had been made accurately and right on time and we sped inland admiring the moonlit scenery and seeing everything in great detail. There was no hint of mist, even in the valleys, as one might have expected. The conditions were quite extraordinary and just as the weathermen had forecast. They must have been pleased with themselves, since even local weather forecasts could be very dodgy during the war when based, as it was, on incomplete information and even worse having to produce it for an area 600 miles away.

The Danish Fields, woods and villages glided peacefully by. The placid rural scenery with its orderly farms and barns was seemingly as far divorced from war as could be imagined. One could easily be lulled into a false sense of security but not for long, since a little later we flew over an army barracks and could see clearly groups of soldiers firing their rifles at us in a vain attempt to stem the tide (although I gave them full marks for trying).

At another point, Ray and I were able to fire several long bursts at an army convoy, we hoped to better effect. We were flying too low for searchlights or light flak to be used against us and the possibility of fighter attack was out of the question. So, for once as gunners we felt the power of being on the offensive, instead of our usual defensive role, on the way to the target. However, before leaving Denmark two long white trails of incendiary bombs could be seen burning on the ground. This was ominous and the indications were that two Lancasters were in trouble - but this is another long story which was confirmed after the war.

The Baltic Sea leg was uneventful although it was amusing and interesting to see red Verey lights being fired as a warning (of us as intruders) to local aircraft when we were flying near their bases. Eventually, the time arrived for us to cross the coast and ascend to 10,000 feet. We were still some distance from Stettin when activity started in the target area.

Flak bursting upwards in plenty; target markers and bombs falling in matching quantity, with the result that fires had already started, when we arrived and the town was getting it "thick and fast".

Tommy dropped his contribution, as far as he could tell spot on a green marker and, satisfied, gave the signal to return home. Perhaps we were a little complacent when suddenly "plink" - on came a master searchlight, followed almost immediately by a ring of possibly 20 or 30 satellite units. We were held in a searchlight cone and flashes on the ground indicated we were in for a heavy barrage.

The flak which came up was concentrated and soon the air was filled with puffs of black smoke to the extent that one could smell it (similar to cordite). Fortunately, the exploding shells were not near enough to cause serious damage but we were taking a fair peppering of shrapnel. A little later I suddenly became aware that the port wing had been holed by light flak and the force of the slipstream was tearing the jagged metal skin.

At the same time poor old Tommy, who had been behind the nose panel when this was partly holed, was forcibly blown backwards against the bulkhead. Although cut about the face and bleeding he was otherwise undamaged. Harry cleaned him up and did his best to plug the hole in the aircraft's nose with a Mae West (!) to avoid heat loss. Luckily for all of us, a 20mm shell which embedded itself in the back of the skipper's seat did not explode. The plane bucked about in reaction to the nearer explosions, but Maurice kept the nose down and by weaving and jinking managed to dodge most of the onslaught. After what seemed to be an age and having lost a lot of height, thankfully we ran out of the searchlights' range.

Apart from the holed wing, the aircraft had received a good deal of superficial damage but overall was judged to be airworthy. The metal skin had ceased tearing and although the damage was situated too near the port flap for comfort, it probably would not affect its operation and efficiency. The loss of height did not matter, since we had to return to ground level anyway. Our course was set westerly and we headed for home over the Baltic Sea.

All was going well but, after a while, we saw a large cargo vessel ahead. We could easily see the ship against its light sea background. On the other hand, we judged that it would be hard for them to see us against a low sky/land horizon and moving quickly. With this advantage, we thought it safe to attack - not that eight .303 Browning peashooters would do all that much damage, but the patter of tiny bullets on their decks might make them hop about a bit. So, being in the advantageous position to judge when the rear gunner and bomb aimer in the front turret would be able to bring their guns to bear on the ship, it was left to me to say when.

The word was duly given and we all fired, but, to our astonishment at the very same moment, the ship's guns opened up with a blast of light flak, the effect of which was like flying down Oxford Street when the Christmas lights are switched on. A very pretty sight it was but not recommended to anyone wishing to live to a ripe old age. Subsequently, Maurice told me that his evasive action, when the ship opened up, was so violent that he nearly had a wing-tip in the water.

He was warned just in time by an Aussie trainee who was acting as a second pilot. Lady Luck was with us at night. A little later we saw another ship. But we dodged this one… We did not report our gunnery exchange at debriefing, though I feel we should have done so as a warning to others. That the raid was a success there was no doubt.

The fires which had started even before we arrived had spread. Smoke had risen to 10,000 feet and the glow of the fires could be seen for at least the first 100 miles of the return journey.

Later reports confirmed that the town centre had been devastated and industrial premises substantially damaged. However, the cost to Bomber Command was also substantial, particularly to Group 1 (our Group). Out of a net 66 Lancasters which took off for the primary target, nine were missing and eleven aircraft were more or less severely damaged. The blast of the war had certainly blown in our ears.

I mentioned earlier that we had carried out low-level flying exercises. Taking these into account plus the low-level attack on Stettin and other subsequent training trips it could be that it was all part of a planned scheme to conceal the activities of Guy Gibson and his Dambusters, who were then training for the special operation in exactly four weeks time on the next full moon."

My father commented about his own experiences of the Stettin raid –

"Although we bombed at 14000 feet, both the outward and

return journey was flown at low level. The outward journey was uneventful, but on return the enemy must have realized that we were flying at low level, as over Denmark I saw up to 6 aircraft shot down by low-level Ack/Ack fire. The site of the North Sea under my wings was eventually a very pleasant relief, to say the least!"

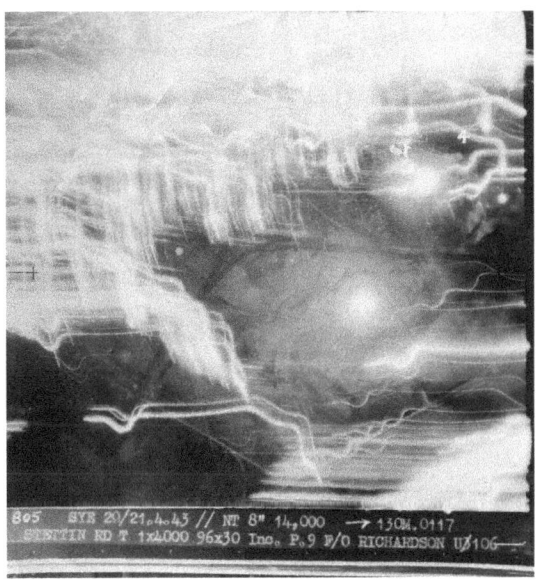

PHOTO TAKEN ON THE STETTIN RAID

GERMAN NIGHT FIGHTERS

"Up to this point in my story, I have not given much information about German night-fighters and other defence tactics employed by ground defences and what steps were taken in an effort to combat them. To Bomber Command crews, German night- fighters were a problem of the first order - a dangerous problem - and the odds of success was stacked in their favour. They had the greatest speed, fire power and manoeuvrability. As if this wasn't enough, they were also assisted by the ground "box" system which effectively vectored them to the desired spot. The German Wurzbung ground radar detectors gave information, which enabled the controllers to put night- fighters into the right position to make interceptions. Again, the greatest problem was that the German night-fighters were aware of the blind spot below British bombers generally, including Lancasters, and were able to use this to their advantage.

The amount of light at horizon level and above varied but a diligent gunner had a good chance of seeing a fighter approaching. However, unless there was 10/10ths cloud say at 10,000 feet and a little moonlight, it was very difficult to see anything in the murk below. Thus, on a moonless night it was an easy ploy for a fighter to slide underneath a bomber and fire (almost) at point blank range. Bomber Command had to live with this situation but a little assistance was obtained by partial jamming of German radar stations by a ground device in this country named "Mandrel".

In addition, a microphone placed in one of the bomber's engines could be tuned by the wireless operator to any frequency on which he heard instructions being broadcast to German pilots. Neither of these systems could cause a breakdown in the German defence but they could, at best interrupt temporarily and, at worst, irritate their operators. With high concentrations of bombers taking part in an air raid, an air gunner was aware, even on the darkest nights, of the presence of other craft within his vicinity.

The question was were the 'black blobs' as they appeared from time to time friend or foe? One became accustomed to concentrating one's sight slightly to the left or right of the "blob" and ignoring direct vision. The eye, at night, can determine features more sharply away from the centre and this method was used to ascertain whether the object under scrutiny had four or two engines. (Because of the location of the optic nerve in the centre rear of the eye.) The latter would, of course indicate the presence of a night-fighter ME 110 or JU-88, (although one had to be careful because at this period some twin-engined Wellington bombers were capable of flying at 20,000 feet).

This system required a good deal of concentration but usually it was only for relatively short periods since bombers did not bunch together for long spells due to several factors, but mainly because of the uncomfortable buffeting, which occurs when flying in the other chap's slipstream. Again, air crew were happier when not flying straight and level, and there was a tendency to weave as much as possible. This made life difficult for the navigator, of course but even more so when a gunner asked for a search below and the pilot would bank steeply one way and then the other in an attempt to spot any fighter lurking in the gloom beneath.

One method of taking evasive action was to "corkscrew". This manoeuvre called for the pilot to fly the plane on a horizontal spiral course. A moving target is always harder to hit and "corkscrewing" was an effective counterattack either from the rear or underneath. However, it had to be used sparingly if rendezvous times were to be achieved."

THE SHEER HELL OF WAR

Dougie concluded his book by stating the following-

"The bombing of German towns was a necessity - it was horrific, evil, and inhuman... it represented the worst elements found in the nature of mankind but it was essential and there was no way of preventing casualties - high casualties in many cases. The Germans used air bombing first. They had no regard for human life.

To those who would criticise ex-servicemen in general and Bomber Command personnel in particular, let me say that I hope they live a pleasant and peaceful life which was assured by the action taken by my generation fifty or so long years ago. The glory of war? To those who think this way, I sincerely hope that they don't have to find out the hard way - it's sheer hell."

DOUGIE AND MAISIE (CHIC) EADES.

My father did his pilots training in Terrell Texas and the following was reported in the Sunderland Echo newspaper –
"Another Wearsider who has just earned his "wings" and received his commission in the U.S.A. is Pilot officer George H.M. Richardson, son of Mr. and Mrs. Richardson of Woodville Crescent, Grindon. The new pilot can hardly be classed as a stranger to the air. His father tells me that he made his first flight at the age of five years old. Educated at Bede school, he entered the R.A.F. at the beginning of the war and went to America for flying training last year. In a recent letter home, he tells of a leave spend on a ranch in Oklahoma, wearing cowboy dress and riding rodeo-trained mustangs over the mountain trails, visiting Red Indians in the camps on their reservations. He seems to have found his wild west adventures almost as thrilling as his first solo flight on advanced trainer planes - a feat which he accomplished on his second day of advanced training."

On arriving in Texas, in October 1941 my father sent a telegram to his mother stating, "All well and safe." The telegram and his subsequent letters during his time in Texas were all sent to:- The Cottage Applegarth, Northallerton, Yorkshire. Presumably, his mother was there with Malcolm his eight year old brother, as Sunderland was heavily bombed during World War II. Both town and port suffered much damage. It was in fact among the seven most bombed towns in Britain. There were 1,367 casualties – 362 were seriously hurt and 267 people killed. Ninety percent of the 34,500 dwellings were damaged of which 2,000 suffered serious damage and 1,013 were a total loss. Shipyards and ports had their share of damage and as a seaport, Sunderland suffered many losses

among her seafaring sons.
One cannot begin to imagine what an anxious time it was from Mary Ann, my grandmother and also for my grandfather. She had gone through 11 pregnancies in order to have three sons and the prospective of them going to war and maybe losing them must have been hard to bear. This scenario was a course repeated by many other families and for some their worst nightmare sadly became reality.

LETTERS FROM TEXAS
The following are three of the letters my father sent to his parents from Terrell Texas –
NO. 1 BRISTISH FLYING TRAINING SCHOOL
ROYAL AIR FORCE
TERRELL, TEXAS, U.S.A.

Sunday 16th November 1941.

Dear Mam,

Well, I still haven't heard from England yet. I'm beginning to wonder whether England still exists. However, there really hasn't been much time yet for anything to arrive from home as it takes about 14 days to get across. Still, I am looking forward to getting one in the near future. You have no idea how dull it is without any letters from home.
Well, I went solo last Tuesday. Much earlier than I expected to. There were 7 of us who went solo on Tuesday morning and I was one of the first three.
I had been flying dual for about 30 minutes and had made

two or three fairly decent take-offs and landings when the instructor climbed out, and said, "Righto! Take her around again, and good luck." Well, I was surprised as I didn't think he had so much confidence in my flying ability. However, I said, "Ok," and took off.

Well, you have no idea what a thrill it is to be flying up there all by yourself. I was excited as can be. I had to land and take off 3 times before it is counted as an official solo. It was great fun. Since then I have done 3 and a half hours solo flying. We use an auxiliary field about 5 miles away now for flying from and I get the job every morning of flying one of the solo-planes across to the field from here, as there are more planes than instructors now that some of us have gone solo.

It is surprising but you feel much more confident without the instructor. Why I don't know, but it is a fact. The only thing that worries me now, is the fact that my stomach has started it's tricks again. I don't think it has properly recovered from the bad time on the boat. Anyway since we have started aero-batics it has been playing tricks. However, I think I am gradually getting used to it. It makes things harder though.

We have just had word that we will probably get 4 days leave for Christmas. I don't think it will be quite enough time to get home though. However we have got more invitations sent to the camp for Christmas than there are chaps on the camp. The hospitality around here is overwhelming.

Tell Malcolm I am sorry to disappoint him but these are there are no cowboys here. In fact we aren't actually on the prairies. Texas is the largest state in the U.S.A. and the prairies start further south-west from here.

The weather here is very changeable. One moment it is hot and the next minute it is quite cold. Somedays it is very windy and yet an hour or so later it is quite calm again. Lately it has been very warm and the heat brings out various different kinds of insects - flies, butterflies (beautiful ones and very big) and of course, mosquitoes. After seeing some of the large variety flying around I am glad we have mosquito netting over the windows and doors. The main crops around here are cotton patches but further south where it is of more consistent weather you will find cowboys, but I'm sorry Malcolm, they don't carry guns anymore. Further south still, Texas borders on Mexico and when I get some leave I hope to get down there if I can. I doubt if I will be allowed to cross the border into Mexico, but I may be able to find some border town with a Mexican atmosphere. Well, Mam, I think I will have to close now, as I have run out of news. All we do here is fly and study and what time we do get off soon passes.

Cheerio for now, and give my love to everybody at home.
Hoping to hear from you soon,
Your loving son, George xxxxxx
P.S Give my kind regards to Mrs Forster & Jack.

8th February 1942

Dear Mam & Dad,

Well, this is Sunday, thank goodness. I have had a very heavy week. On top of the normal weeks flying, we have had night flying on three of the nights this week. Consequently, I am having a quiet weekend this time. I didn't go to Cooper because the Millers have gone away on a business deal this week. Instead I just stayed in camp and went out on Saturday night to the pictures in Terrell. The picture was "Target for Tonight." I have seen it before but I still enjoyed it. It is a good picture.

Today I am just lounging about taking things easy and I will probably go to a show again tonight. I didn't go for breakfast until 10a.m. this morning. I was lucky to get it.

I am feeling quite fit now. The incision is just a thin red scar now and it is gradually getting whiter. It doesn't affect me at all and I am feeling better now then I felt before the operation. Night flying, by the way, is really good fun. It is like floating over a fairyland of lights.

The last time I was up we cruised around for about 25 minutes and then practiced landings for about 30 minutes. I hope to do some solo night flying soon.

I was at Cooper last weekend and had a really good time. I knew that later in the week I should be going on a cross-country flight to Sulphur Springs, so the Milllers asked me to fly over Cooper which is quite near to Sulphur Springs and do some aerobatics. However, as I left Sulphur Springs to return to Terrell an instructor was leaving at the same time so I had to fly straight back. I expect the Millers were disappointed. We're going on a much longer cross-country this week and I am really looking forward to it. I get fed up with the flying near the 'drone practicing various manoeuvres. I like to fly to different places. After all that's what an aeroplane is for.

I'm enclosing some photographs which some of the boys of taken. One is of the barracks and the two of the aeroplane are the type of plane I am changing over to in about 4 weeks time.

Quite nice planes. I have written one or two remarks on the backs. Well I don't think I have any more news, so I will have to close.
By the way I haven't heard from you since Christmas.

Well, cheerio for now,

Your loving son, George. xxxxxxxx

P.S. Give my love to everybody at home.
(The operation my father referred to was an appendectomy.)

Tuesday 24th February 1942

Dear Mam and Dad,

I must apologise for not having written for about ten days, but we have been flying night and day for the last fortnight, and I haven't been able to write any letters at all.
I have 81 flying hours in now and have gone solo on night flying. I have 5 hours dual and 2 hours solo night flying. I will get another hour in tomorrow night. It is good fun.
I have done 12 and three quarter hours cross-country flying having flown to Sulphur Springs twice (50 miles away) and back, Paris (65 miles away) and back, Greenville, Wills Point, and back to Terrell (a triangular flight which I have done twice) and lastly to Gainsville and back, the longest one of the lot (82 miles away). Oh no! There is one more - to Sherman and back (about 70 miles away). In other words, close on

1000 miles cross-country flying. I am getting quite good on navigating now.

Today I did 40 minutes solo formation flying. That was good fun as well. They were three of us flying in V formation with an instructor leading us in the front 'plane.

When you change positions at the back of the V (in other words, the other two back planes change over) the right one goes underneath and the left one goes over the top and take up opposite positions. It is grand doing that. One moment I was on the right and the next moment I was on the left.

After I have got another 10 hours in I go on to Basic 'planes (I am enclosing a photo of one with "yours truly" sitting inside like a lord), but first of all we get 8 days leave. I'm either going to stay at Cooper and they will take me around the races at Hot Springs, Oklahoma, and the rodeo at Fort Worth - these are some of the places they have promised to take me or else I'm going with some of the boys on a tour of New Mexico etc.

I may be able to do both as we are not due to finish until a week come Saturday. Well, as it will not take us long to get 10 hours in we should be finished by this weekend and probably get more leave. However, I will let you know how I get on.

I got your telegram today, by the way, and thanks very much. I am pleased you receive my letter ok. I am absolutely A1 and the incision is just a faint red line now.

In a week or two's time I shall be able to play football etc. again. I'm not going to though, as I intend to rest myself for a good few months yet. I'm not taking any chances. I feel a lot better now than I felt before I had the operation.

I received a letter from auntie Nellie last week so tell her I will answer it as soon as I get a chance.

Well, Mam and Dad, I think that is all the news I have, so cheerio for now and give my love to everyone at home,
Your loving son, George xxxxxxx

THE NORMANDEE

On reaching New York on his way to Texas, my father saw and took photos of the Normandee ship. This was a beautiful French ship that was hailed as beautiful outside but in the interior no expense had been spared and it was apparently quite magnificent, especially the dining room but even more importantly The Normandee had won the prestigious Blue Riband award for speed. She was only four and a half years old when she was laid up in New York at Pier 8, and while being converted to a navy troopship for Allied service, she caught fire just days before the start of World War II and later capsized.

THE NORMANDEE

OBSERVATIONS REGARDING FEAR

My father made some interesting observations regarding fear whilst flying –

"I found that just before take-off was the time when fear came in, - or perhaps some would call it apprehension. What is the difference? All I know is that something clutched at your heart and made it beat faster. I did not notice any others showing fear, but I would be surprised if they did not have similar feelings akin to mine. Once in the air, however, there was so much to cope with and occupy one's mind, that any fear seemed to take second place, and, in any case, training disciplines took over. However, my time of greatest fear and stress was not on ops., but while at O.T.U., - flying those clapped out Whitleys. On two occasions, in atrocious weather conditions at night, I had engine trouble. On the first occasion I had a problem shortly after take off. The starboard engine cut out, and no sooner had I trimmed the aircraft to fly one engine, when it started up again, causing the plane to nearly go out of control. This happened about half a dozen times, and during that time my altitude varied between 6000 feet and 2000 feet! Not a very pleasant thought in the mountains of Scotland!

I was loathe to feather the starboard engine as the thought of landing on one engine did not appeal to me, although I realized that a fluctuating engine could be even more dangerous. Eventually, I did approach the aerodrome with the two engines functioning, only to be met by a RED light! But that is another story.

Two days later, I took off on another night cross country flight, again in atrocious weather, when the same thing happened. The starboard engine cut out. I was directed to Silloth, where they proceeded to bring me down by BEEM APPROACH. In 1942 this system was hardly out of the science fiction scene and consequently very hit and miss. It was like sitting in the LINK TRAINER with only instruments to fly by (we were flying in 10/10 cloud), only this time you had the extra "help" of dots and dashes etc. ringing in your ears to guide, and a running commentary from the tower. And, of course, a fluctuating starboard engine thrown in! I have never had a shirt so soaked in perspiration! Ops., in comparison, were relatively easy as far as fear was concerned. How I appreciated then, the value of good, rigorous training, and the disciplines that go with it. I also appreciated the efforts of the control tower. They did an excellent job. According to my logbook this episode took 3 and a quarter hours."

As mentioned earlier in the excerpt from Dougie Eades book, my parents, George and Dereen married during the war. Their wedding day was on October 3rd 1942 in St Luke's Church

Torquay. The vicar was the Reverend A.G. Backhouse whom my father said was a nephew of the person who bequeathed Backhouse Park to Sunderland.

My father was posted to Wimslow on the same day as the wedding, so Rev. Backhouse saw the Railway Transport Officer (R.T.O.) who made sure they had a locked carriage all to themselves.

During his service in World War II, some of the places my father was posted to included Newark, Devon, Gloucestershire and Kinloss, Scotland.

My mother was only aged 19 when war broke out and her sweetheart, George was needed to fight the war. She chose to join the war effort by offering her services to The Women's Auxiliary Air Force (the W.A.A.F.) where she also served after her marriage until she became pregnant. Her discharge certificate states that her rank was a "leading aircraftswoman" and that she was a telephonist.

She is described as being 5 feet 2 and a half inches in height, having brown hair and eyes and a fair complexion. Comments regarding her work by her squadron leader state that she was a "keen and intelligent airwoman; neat and tidy in appearance at all times, a conscientious worker" and "suitable for re-enrolment."

She gave birth to my sister, Deanne on November 10th 1943 at her parents' home 29 Dunbar Street, Sunderland.

Unfortunately during this year my father was having trouble with his legs and was diagnosed with multiple sclerosis, so had to leave active service.

In my father's own words -

"The M.S. first reared its head while I was stationed at St. Eval,

Cornwall. We did three ops. (anti – submarine strikes), in Whitleys, over the Bay of Biscay, and it was during this time but I noticed that I was dragging my left leg. The M.O. thought that it could be a "flat foot" problem and strapped my foot and leg with elasticated bandages to support the arch of my foot, and I carried on flying. Later, at Syerston (106 squadron) my walk deteriorated so much that I began to use a cycle to get about. The final crunch came when we were doing fighter affiliation. During the changeover of pilots, I was thrown down the fuselage of the plane, and when we landed I had to be half carried to the sick bay. From then on it was hospitals etc. etc. with an eventual diagnosis of M.S. (or disseminated sclerosis as it was called in those days). No more flying!"

A SAD END TO OUR CREW

The crew my father flew with continued with a different pilot and Gordon Brake from Croydon, who was the navigator was replaced. He was about twenty five years of age at that time and was posted elsewhere. Sadly, the rest of the crew lost their lives in August 1943, not long after Gordon and my father left them. Their ages varied from 20 to 28 years of age when they last flew with my father. He said that they were a great crew and that he was privileged to work with them – **Alec Blazer** aged 21 from Mitcham Surrey, **"Ginger" Dawson** aged 20 from Littleborough, Lancashire, **Peter Moxham** aged 28, Johnny Wardle aged 20 from Palmers Green, London and **Peter Henderson** aged 20 – a volunteer from Southern Ireland. Gordon wrote to my father – "It is a sad end to our crew. Who knows – it might have been different if we could have stayed with them. That is something we can never know."

11

GEORGE AND DEREEN AND FAMILY LIFE

Their first family home together was 10 The Oaks in Sunderland after having lived at 29 Dunbar Street with Dereen's parents for nearly a year and then with George's parents at 29 Woodville Crescent. 10 The Oaks is a large six bedroomed house and the family occupied the entire ground floor with others renting the rest of the house. My sister remembers the lovely bay window and that there was a very long corridor leading to the kitchen. She was two years old when they arrived at The Oaks. She attended the Montessori School where her father had once been a pupil and was surrounded by loving relatives on both sides of her family.

On his National Registration Identity Card, my father is recorded as being a Traffic Movement Officer, employed by The Ministry of War Department in May 1944.

I remember our parents recounting an interesting story about my sister when they were living at The Oaks. One day when she was riding her tricycle outside the house there was a knock on the door and when our mother answered it, there stood a not-very-happy lady who happened to be an alderman's wife, which apparently gave her some standing in the town.

My sister was standing next to her with her tricycle. The lady said to our mother, "This child went into me on her tricycle and has laddered my stockings!" (Apparently stockings were still very expensive even though the war had finished). My mother turned to my sister and asked her, "Why did you do this?" To which she replied, "I did ring my bell and she didn't get out of the way!" (Deanne grew up to marry and her family relocated to Australia for many decades. She has two wonderful sons, Dominic and Matthew).

MIGRATING SOUTH

My parents George and Dereen moved hundreds of miles down to South East Kent when my sister was six and a half years old and our mother was pregnant with me where our father had been offered a good job as a traffic superintendent with British Road Services (B.R.S.) a prominent road haulage company at that time. (Subsequently, he would become a branch manager and later in his life, a church minister). However, we made regular trips to the northeast where both sets of grandparents still lived along with other relatives.

LEFT TO RIGHT - Dereen, Uncle John, Auntie Nellie with my sister on her knee, Uncle Malcolm, Nanna Richardson and Grandpa Richardson.

GEORGE AND DEREEN ON THEIR WEDDING DAY IN TORQUAY IN 1942 DURING THE SECOND WORLD WAR.

AUNTIE NELLIE WITH UNCLE MALCOLM AND MY SISTER.

12
MEMORIES OF THE NORTH EAST & RELATIVES

I loved going to the northeast. Sunderland, and the surrounding area where both sets of grandparents, as well as other relatives, lived was like Wonderland to me and it felt like home as we were so much loved and welcomed. I remember feeling excited on the journey up as we approached Doncaster with only a hundred miles to go, and soon the orange lights of the northeast would appear. (Back in the South they were a yellowish colour). The M1 had not yet been built so the journey of some 350 miles could take a long time. I remember on one occasion when it was very foggy, it took us 13 hours.

The people in the North East seemed warmer than in the South. I liked the way Nanna Richardson and Auntie Nellie used to refer to our father as "our George" or my uncles as "our Roy" and "our Malcolm." This was not common down South.

It also felt good when my sister and I were called "the bairns" and where everyone seemed to call each other "Pet," and later, when I was older, my grandfather used to call me "Pet Hinny," Hinny, being a name for a young lass or girl.

When shopping for sweets, if I was a bit short of the money needed for an item, the shopkeeper would invariably say, "Never mind Pet," and let me have the sweets! This never happened down South.

MY MOTHER'S BROTHERS AND SISTER
At Seaham Harbour, now known as Seaham, Uncle Sid, my

mother's eldest brother used to introduce me to neighbours and friends saying, "This is my niece, Hilary. She lives in the South and talks posh!" I didn't feel that I spoke posh. I just spoke like others who lived in Canterbury but I wished that I had a north-eastern accent like my parents (especially like my mother who had a more pronounced accent than my father) and the rest of my relatives in the North East as it sounded much more interesting and friendly than what I felt was the rather cold accent of the South.

However, I have to admit that Sunderland, like London in those days was actually a very dirty place as it was very industrial. You only had to be there a day and your clothes were very grimy, especially around the collar. Households in those days did not burn smokeless fuel and Sunderland was still the biggest shipbuilding town in the whole world. However, there was something about the ships on the River Wear that fascinated me and I felt glad to be associated with such a place.

Uncle Sid was in the building trade and after his son, my cousin Jimmy, who was in the navy, brought me back a doll, Uncle Sid offered to make me a doll's cot.

He looked at the doll and said, "Now let me see - that would be about three bricks long." "Oh no!" I replied, "I don't want a brick doll's cot". Uncle Sid started to laugh and said, "I was only talking about bricks to assess the size needed." "Of course, your cot will be made of wood!"

My granddaughter, Mila now has this cot that her great, great Uncle Sid made!

Uncle Sid was married to Auntie Ella and they had two sons, David and James or Jimmy.

My mother's other brother Arthur was married to Marianne

12

MEMORIES OF THE NORTH EAST & RELATIVES

I loved going to the northeast. Sunderland, and the surrounding area where both sets of grandparents, as well as other relatives, lived was like Wonderland to me and it felt like home as we were so much loved and welcomed. I remember feeling excited on the journey up as we approached Doncaster with only a hundred miles to go, and soon the orange lights of the northeast would appear. (Back in the South they were a yellowish colour). The M1 had not yet been built so the journey of some 350 miles could take a long time. I remember on one occasion when it was very foggy, it took us 13 hours.

The people in the North East seemed warmer than in the South. I liked the way Nanna Richardson and Auntie Nellie used to refer to our father as "our George" or my uncles as "our Roy" and "our Malcolm." This was not common down South.

It also felt good when my sister and I were called "the bairns" and where everyone seemed to call each other "Pet," and later, when I was older, my grandfather used to call me "Pet Hinny," Hinny, being a name for a young lass or girl.

When shopping for sweets, if I was a bit short of the money needed for an item, the shopkeeper would invariably say, "Never mind Pet," and let me have the sweets! This never happened down South.

MY MOTHER'S BROTHERS AND SISTER

At Seaham Harbour, now known as Seaham, Uncle Sid, my

mother's eldest brother used to introduce me to neighbours and friends saying, "This is my niece, Hilary. She lives in the South and talks posh!" I didn't feel that I spoke posh. I just spoke like others who lived in Canterbury but I wished that I had a north-eastern accent like my parents (especially like my mother who had a more pronounced accent than my father) and the rest of my relatives in the North East as it sounded much more interesting and friendly than what I felt was the rather cold accent of the South.

However, I have to admit that Sunderland, like London in those days was actually a very dirty place as it was very industrial. You only had to be there a day and your clothes were very grimy, especially around the collar. Households in those days did not burn smokeless fuel and Sunderland was still the biggest shipbuilding town in the whole world. However, there was something about the ships on the River Wear that fascinated me and I felt glad to be associated with such a place.

Uncle Sid was in the building trade and after his son, my cousin Jimmy, who was in the navy, brought me back a doll, Uncle Sid offered to make me a doll's cot.

He looked at the doll and said, "Now let me see - that would be about three bricks long." "Oh no!" I replied, "I don't want a brick doll's cot". Uncle Sid started to laugh and said, "I was only talking about bricks to assess the size needed." "Of course, your cot will be made of wood!"

My granddaughter, Mila now has this cot that her great, great Uncle Sid made!

Uncle Sid was married to Auntie Ella and they had two sons, David and James or Jimmy.

My mother's other brother Arthur was married to Marianne

and they had a son called Geoffrey. I remember Uncle Arthur being a very kind and generous man. They lived in Sunderland until Geoffrey was seventeen when they moved down south.

My Auntie Gladys, my mother's only sister married a Southerner, Uncle Ron and they lived in London. They had two children Michael and Patricia. Despite the age gap of over five years, Gladys and my mother were very close. Auntie Gladys often told me that they were best friends as well as sisters. Auntie Gladys lived into her mid-90s and after her husband died she relocated to Devon to be near his sisters. One time when I visited her when she was in her eighties, she told me of an interesting experience she'd had.

She said that she hadn't thought of praying for years since she'd been at school. However, she had reached a stage in her life when she felt she'd had enough of being on this earth, so this one particular night she had thought, "God, I don't want to wake up tomorrow." She went to sleep and woke up in the middle of the night and her bedroom was filled with light.

She pinched herself to see if she was dreaming and it hurt! The next thing that happened was that she seemed to be in a long queue but she didn't know what she was queueing for, so she thought to herself, "I need to find out!" She gingerly started to walk down the side of the queue and was very surprised that no one stopped her. On arriving at the front of the queue, there stood a man who, she said, looked at her with such eyes of love that she had never experienced before. She knew it was Jesus. He put His hand on her shoulder and said, "Gladys, you must go back. Your time is not yet."

GRANDPARENTS

Christmas at Nanna and Grandpa Richardson's was always a sumptuous affair. Her sister, Auntie Nellie joined her in giving everyone the most amazing food. We loved Sasparella (a fizzy drink a bit like Dandelion and Burdock) and the delicious homemade bread which Nanna cut into wafer-thin slices.

However, her butter rich ice-cream was amazing in the days when very few people owned a fridge or freezer. Auntie Nellie with her mother, Jane (who bought my father his first car) used to have their own bakery and cake shop in Tateham Street, Sunderland. My sister remembers great-grandmother Jane Merchant and liked to play with her musical box but she had died by the time I came along.

Nanna and Grandpa Richardson always seemed to have the latest gadgets in contrast to Nanna and Grandpa Saunders who, being older, and their children all grown were more old-fashioned. They lived in different homes during my childhood, but my favourite was a modern house on a corner in Leominster Road, Sunderland where Uncle Malcolm lived with them before his marriage and Grandpa created a beautiful garden.

It was always a treat to visit Grandpa and Nanna Saunders. Grandpa was an interesting conversationalist. Their two-bedroomed home at 29 Dunbar Street, the street being still cobbled, was a double-fronted terraced bungalow which is very common in the northeast. The left-hand front room was a bedroom and the right-hand front room was the lounge or parlour. Both were accessed from the hallway which led to the main living/dining room. The second bedroom was accessed on the right of this room. The decor and furniture were very old-fashioned. They didn't have a bathroom but used a tin bath for bathing. The toilet was accessed from the yard outside and was part of the small building which housed the coal. The kitchen felt more like a corridor which led off the living room to the outside yard. They didn't have a washing machine but they used a washboard to help clean the clothes and a mangle to squeeze the water out.

I remember staying there and sleeping in the front parlour. I remember thinking there was a rather foreboding feel about the room. It was very old-fashioned with a very large settee and chairs. Two of the chairs were put together for me to sleep in.

As I went to sleep I felt almost as if I was living in an earlier time.

SUNDERLAND HOUSING

There was an interesting report done in 1906 regarding the housing in Sunderland for working men and their families. It stated that there were three types of housing. The first being the old tenement buildings mainly in the East End of the town which were once the homes of wealthy families, but now housed four or more families. Residents included shipyard labourers and dock workers. The second type of housing were purpose built properties for letting out as tenements. Weekly rent ranged from one shilling and sixpence to two shillings for one room to eight shillings for five rooms. Unskilled workers rarely paid more than three shillings and sixpence to four shillings while rents of seven shillings or more were paid by foremen or other higher wage earners. The third type of housing was the terraced cottages described in this chapter and these were often owner occupied and favoured by skilled craftsman in the shipyards. Council houses replaced the overcrowded tenements of the East End in the early 1900s.

GREAT UNCLE JOHN AND AUNTIE NELLIE

Uncle John and Auntie Nellie's terraced bungalow at 17 Hastings Street, in the Hendon district of Sunderland, had a different layout to Nanna and Grandpa Saunders' home. It had an indoor bathroom and was not double-fronted but went further back. It still had two bedrooms. Inside the hallway to the right was the front parlour and at the end of the hall on the right was the door to the living/ dining room with a bedroom leading off to the left. There was another bedroom with a bathroom leading off it behind the living room.

The kitchen was to the left of this bedroom and had a glass roof to give some light through to the living room window. In the yard, there was a back gate leading to a wide cobbled thoroughfare which the whole street backed onto and also had access to the back of the next street. They also had a television which was relatively early for those days.

I remember the volume was very loud and wondered why because they didn't seem old enough to be deaf. However, as I now think about it, Uncle John worked as a plater in the shipyards where it was very noisy which may have caused hearing loss. He was a man who even though we did not share a bloodline, always made me feel as if I belonged to him. I remember them coming to stay with us down South and he liked to play with our cat Sooty. We went to a carnival and he won a doll for me. He was very generous and kind and liked to slip me some money to buy sweets.

He had married late after the second World War in 1945, when he was 44 and Auntie Nellie was 49. They had been courting for some time I believe, but Uncle John was looking after his elderly mother. When she died, they married in July 1945 at

the end of World War II and he moved in with Auntie Nellie who was living with her mother, Jane at 17 Hastings Street.
They continued to live there after Jane Merchant died three years later in 1948. Aunty Nellie was a strong, gutsy, northern lady. As a child, I was a bit in awe of her. She spoke her mind which some see as a northern trait and could be quite forceful in her opinions if she felt something wasn't right. Like my grandmother, she was very generous. Apart from always having a seemingly endless supply of KitKats in her sideboard cupboard, her cooking was amazing and she often gave me money for sweets and I remember her buying me some boots. She cared about people in general.
Later, as a teenager, I went back up north to live. My plan was to live with Grandpa Saunders who was on his own after Nanna Saunders had died. Unfortunately, he died alone the year before I had finished my nursery nursing training. My other grandfather, Grandpa Richardson having married again was now back living in Sunderland. I found a job with accommodation at a residential nursery. I felt that I belonged in the North East and that it was going to be my home from then on and I had no interest of ever living in the South again.
I stayed with Auntie Nellie and Uncle John on a regular basis and realised that although she could seem tough on the outside Auntie Nellie had a very soft centre. I knew that she would always "fight my corner" if necessary and she helped fill the gap left by my mother and grandmother, her sister. She treated me as if I was her own child. She was very generous. As recorded earlier, my father always used to say that he and his siblings felt as though they had three mothers – their biological mother Mary, their Auntie Nellie and their grandmother Jane and

Auntie Nellie was like another grandmother to me.

Uncle John was heartbroken after Auntie Nellie died. She was the strong one and his rock. I visited him sometime after but he didn't answer the door - maybe he didn't hear! I went back again with Nicola and Andrew, our children. This time I was more persistent and banged for some time. He finally answered and let us in. I was very moved by what I saw.

The once vibrant house was in decay with wallpaper peeling off. Uncle John looked as if he had given up on life. However, he seemed to cheer up as we chatted. The next time I saw him, he was in a care home. It was one of the best that I have visited, with cheerful staff and residents and Uncle John seemed much happier.

The last time I saw Uncle John was in hospital in Newcastle a few days before he died. As I had a young family to care for, I was not able to spend much time away from home so I took the overnight coach from East Kent and spent the morning with him before catching the coach back at lunchtime. He was so glad to see me but when I went to say goodbye, tears filled his eyes and looking around him, his eyes fell upon a wad of green paper towels by his bedside. He gave them to me saying, "Here you are, Pet, you have these from me!" Even in his last illness, he wasn't thinking of himself but wanted to give me something. I took the paper towels feeling that I was stealing from the hospital but I couldn't refuse him because I knew he would be very hurt. Here was a man who had been in the centre of a happy family and friends, who had travelled abroad and had a full life. Those friends and close relatives had either died or gone to live away. There have been and there are so many like him.

UNCLE JOHN'S UNION CARD

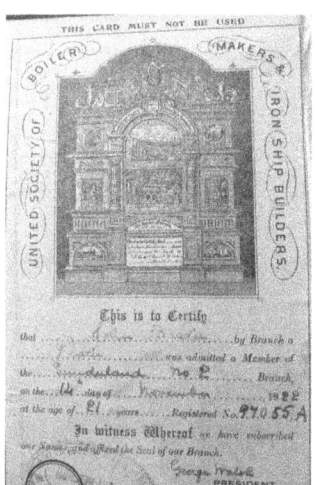

MY FATHER'S BROTHERS

I remember one summer holiday in Sunderland, going to the beach at Roker or Seaburn. It was quite hot and suddenly, we heard the welcome sound of an ice cream van. In those days ice cream vans often travelled to where people gathered and also went round peoples' homes.

These vehicles had loudspeakers and played jingly type music as they approached. I remember being happy about being able to have an ice cream but was even more excited when I saw that the ice cream man was, in fact, my Uncle Malcolm, my father's youngest brother. He was nearly 15 years younger than my father and was only ten when my sister was born. He was on vacation from Durham University where he was doing dentistry.

I was much more impressed that he was an ice cream man than the fact he was going to be a dentist. I wasn't very keen on dentists because when I'd had a tooth out, the anaesthetic gas I was given made me ill. It wasn't long after Uncle Malcolm qualified that I needed another extraction and as we were going to Sunderland, it was decided that he would treat me. The word "treat" sounds fun but it wasn't for me!

With the dentist at home, as I didn't really know him and found him a bit intimidating, I didn't dare make too much fuss, but with Uncle Malcolm, however, it was a different story! He had to chase me around the surgery to even get me to sit in the chair, and yes, it was horrible! I had a nightmare dream under the anaesthetic and felt sick and ill for some time after. It was probably a baptism of fire for newly qualified Uncle Malcolm. (Although my sister has told me that he used to practice on her before he was qualified!).

I found Uncle Malcolm very interesting, probably partly due to the fact that he was my youngest uncle and also because he was good at telling stories.

I remember him at home with my grandparents during his university holidays playing recordings of the latest songs at that time such as *"I Am A Mole and I Live in a Hole"* *"I'm Just An Old Fashioned Girl"* and *"Downtown"* by Petula Clark.

Uncle Malcolm later relocated to Spain with his wife Jill and our cousins, James and Marie-Claire.

Uncle Roy, my father's other brother was married to Auntie Jean and they had a son David who relocated to the States. Unlike his siblings, who both had dark hair, Uncle Roy was quite blonde. He used to tell a lot of jokes which I thought were great. However, I did see his wife, Auntie Jean sometimes roll her eyes. I suppose she had heard them all before!

13

HOPE AND HEARTACHE

After a few years of living in the South East, when I was about four and a half years old, my parents were to have an experience that would change the course of their lives. Billy Graham's visit to London in 1954 led to them becoming committed practising Christians. I remember my mother was very excited about her newfound faith. She would say that she'd always thought that Christianity was just for "goodie goodies" (an expression at that time) but realised that it was for everyone who knew that they needed Jesus. He then would change their lives.

She used to go around the house singing a hymn, *Blessed Assurance, Jesus, is mine. This is my story, this is my song, praising my Saviour all the day long*. She had always seemed a cheerful person to me and had a good sense of humour, but even to my young eyes, I could see something wonderful had happened to her!

One day when I was 10 years old, my father, sister and I waved goodbye to my mother, before going our separate ways to school and work. I remember her coming to the end of the drive and standing there until I was out of sight. Unbeknown to me, this was to be the last time that I would see her on this earth.

That afternoon a family friend from our church came to pick me up from school and take me home in his car. This seemed unusual as I always went home on the bus with the other children from our district, but all the same, I was very excited when I saw him as I was very fond of him. On arriving home, I was told that my mother was dead.

My first reaction was one of disbelief! To my childish mind, this was not possible! People I knew who had died, were either ill, old or had been in some sort of accident and my mother did not fit into any of these categories. She had apparently just dropped down dead in the middle of Canterbury while out shopping.

I wasn't told the cause of her death until I was almost an adult and was considered too young to go to the funeral so these emissions did not help me to come to terms with her death over the following years. In the early days after her death, I even wondered if she had left us for some reason and she hadn't really died.

I remember receiving more presents than usual – some from people who would not normally give me presents that first Christmas without her. It was very kind of them but as I opened them all, I just kept thinking that all I wanted was Mummy.

A family friend told my father she had been speaking with my mother in Canterbury not long before she died. They had been talking of various things that were happening around the world and she recorded that my mother concluded the conversation by saying, "There is no real lasting peace outside Jesus!" These were to be her last known words on this earth.

BILLY GRAHAM

Billy Graham was an American with Scottish ancestry who first came to Britain in 1954. He encountered much skepticism at first but went on to preach to thousands at London's Harringay and Wembley arenas, meet Winston Churchill and at one of the meetings Geoffrey Fisher, the Archbishop of Canterbury gave the benediction.

Over the ensuing years, Billy and his wife, Ruth were regular guests of Queen Elizabeth and Billy preached at both Windsor and Sandringham.

In December 2001, Queen Elizabeth conferred on Billy Graham an honorary Knighthood as a Knight Commander of the Most Excellent Order of the British Empire. Honorary knighthoods, apart from the exchange of honours with heads of State, are sparingly given.

In 2022, during Queen Elizabeth's last days, when talking about her faith, she mentioned to Ian Greenshields, (then the Moderator of the General Assembly of the Church of Scotland) about an American religious leader who she said had made a big impact on her. This must have been Billy Graham as there is no record of her meeting any other American spiritual leader on such a regular basis.

Billy came to Sunderland in the 1980s (as part of a tour of several towns and cities) and preached at Roker Park stadium. I took my children to see him. He was then in his sixties. The district was affected by the miners' strike at that time and he made a point of meeting a group of unemployed men who were very impressed with him. He referred in his preaching what he had learned from them about their frustrations and difficulties. It was very cold while Billy was in Sunderland with rain and a biting wind. Billy recalled years later, "I had a heavy suit and the heaviest coat I could get, I had a scarf around my neck while I was singing, and I had a hat on for the first time in my life preaching. I was so cold I could hardly get my mouth opened!" There was a greater response in terms of the percentage of people attending the meetings at Sunderland when Billy invited people to become Christians than any of the other places he visited in England that year.

In 1984, Billy preached in a chilly wind and below-freezing temperatures Sunderland, England, near the North Sea.

MEMORIES OF MY MOTHER DEREEN

Unfortunately, I only knew my mother for the first ten years of my life. After my guests had departed on my tenth birthday party, I went into the lounge where she opened out her arms to me. I cuddled into her and she said, "Ee, you're getting older! You're double figures now!"

The following is what I remember about her - She was warm and gave lovely cuddles. I knew she loved my sister and I very much. She was dark-haired with brown eyes and just over 5-ft 2 in height. Her northeastern accent was more pronounced than my father's.

She loved nature – birds, animals and flowers. We would go to the woods, primrose picking and at Easter rolled painted eggs down the hill, often meeting up with her sister, Gladys and family. She used to watch the birds in the garden using her great-grandfather James's binoculars. She loved our cat who was named Sooty because he was black. He had long hair with big yellow eyes. He was a very soft cat and allowed her to use him as a stole around her neck. She hoovered his tummy! In those days, vacuum cleaners were not as powerful! We would dress Sooty up in my baby clothes and she would sit with him on the garden swing! Looking back, he was a rather remarkable cat, as most cats would run away rather than suffer all that we did to him!

During the last holiday we had in Wales, she loved the mountains and we were planning to go to Austria the next year. My father decided we needed a new car and she said she would like one that was cream with red leather seats and he happily obliged. It was an Austin A50 with an A55 engine, which I remember her driving occasionally. There weren't many women drivers in those days.

From a child's perspective, she could be great fun! We had a silly game when I was small where she would say, "Goodnight, my little lamb" and I would reply, "Goodnight, mother sheep" and we would go through all the animals I could think of and then she would say, "nighty nighty" and I would say, "pyjamas pyjamas" and she would say, "slippers slippers" and I would say, "dressing gown, dressing gown" etc. – anything to keep her there!

I remember her with my sister and I painting the threadbare dining room carpet with some pencils that painted which I'd had one birthday. Sometimes we played a game where we sang everything rather than saying it - such as at the table we would sing, "Pass the sugar" etc. Invariably, on the first day of a month, she would gently punch and pinch me saying, "Pinch, punch, first day of the month." In return, I would give her a gentle pinch and kick saying, "A nip and a kick for being so quick!"

Dereen loved her garden and grew peas, runner beans, strawberries, raspberries, marrows, blackcurrants, gooseberries, potatoes, lettuce, carrots, radishes, apples, rhubarb, cherries and flowers such as lilac, standard rose trees, rockeries, lavender, peonies, weigela, rockery plants, daffodils, tulips and cornflowers. She bottled much of her produce for us to consume over the winter months. We also picked wild blackberries which she made into delicious blackberry jelly.

She was very nurturing especially when I was ill. I remember the first day in recovery was spent inside, the second day we went outside for a walk and it wasn't until the third day of feeling better I was allowed back to school.

She liked watching Russ Conway playing the piano on TV. She was also fond of westerns and I remember her watching Emma by Jane Austin.

She liked history. She told me about a visit to York when she was a child and seemed very excited about the street called The Shambles which was so narrow that people could shake hands with people from the houses opposite.

My mother had a really good sense of humour! On the last holiday, we all had together in North Wales, there was a waitress at The Riverside Hotel Pennal, where we were staying. Her name was Bernadette and she had an interesting accent and spoke very slowly and rather lethargically! For example, I remember her asking us, "Do you want sope it's pay, green pay?" ("Do you want soup, it's pea, green pea?" – as if peas could be any other colour than green!) My mother would wait until she reckoned Bernadette was out of earshot and mimic her, "Do you want sope, it's pay, green pay?" We would all burst out laughing except my father who I felt wasn't too keen on us drawing attention to ourselves in the hotel dining room!

My mother (Dereen) is sitting on the left, my sister on the right, my father is standing on the right and I am on the left at the front.
OUR FAMILY WITH FRIENDS WE MADE AT OUR LAST FAMILY HOLIDAY AT THE RIVERSIDE HOTEL PENNAL, NORTH WALES.

SOOTY.

CHILDHOOD MEMORIES OF MY FATHER

My father was an interesting man. Being the eldest of three boys, he was, like some firstborns more serious than his brothers. However, life with him did have its lighter moments. He and my mother were obviously well-matched and after her death, some neighbours and relatives commented on how obvious their love for each other was.

I grew up aware of this. Every wedding anniversary he would buy red roses for her and most weeks he would come home from work with a small box of Cadbury's Milk Tray chocolates. They were also quite tactile with each other. There were songs from their youth that they liked such as "Do You Remember - Sweetheart, Sweetheart, Sweetheart." from the musical Maytime.

When I was quite small I would stand on his feet while he walked around and he would tickle my tummy with his moustache. Later, he allowed me to tap dance on the kitchen floor wearing his precious cowboy boots which he bought during the war when he was doing pilot training in Texas.

As my sister was so much older than me, and in common with many others in those days, I did not go to nursery school, in my preschool days I invented an imaginary friend - Penguin! I'm sure it was very inconvenient for my parents especially when I burst into tears when someone sat next to me and I told them that they had sat on Penguin.

One day my father decided it was time for Penguin to go! He told me that Penguin wanted to explore the world and pretended to take him by the hand, (or flipper!) then took him to the front door and said, "Goodbye Penguin." He came back into the lounge where I was sitting and said, "Penguin has gone on his travels and he is very happy." I looked at my father and said, "Oh no you're wrong! He changed his mind. He would never leave me." My father said, "I'm afraid he has gone. I let him out of the front door!" To which I replied, "Well he is right next to me because he returned through the back door!"

Later, during my school holidays, my father would come home from his office for lunch and I would race up to the top of our road which was a cul-de-sac and on a hill and he would let me sit on his lap and steer the car down the road to our house.

He was very good at table tennis and although he wrote with his right hand he would hold the bat in his left hand and spin the ball so that it was almost impossible to return it. I also used to enjoy playing crazy golf with him on holiday.

Although less demonstrative than our mother, I knew that he loved us and when I had childhood illnesses he would bring me presents that he had purchased after work. Presents, I particularly liked were a Pelham puppet and a kaleidoscope. I really appreciated these presents as I knew he had chosen and bought them by himself rather than the Christmas and birthday presents which I reckoned my mother had bought.

Our aforementioned cat, Sooty, was quite a clever cat! My father didn't allow Sooty to go upstairs. During the daytime when my father was at work, Sooty would often either sleep in my old carrycot under my bed or in the airing cupboard. Around six o'clock, my father's key would go in the front door and Sooty would be downstairs in a flash before my father could see him! However, many years later my father told me that he did know what Sooty was up to.

I loved hearing my father play the piano. There was a freedom of spirit about him as he played that wasn't always evident in everyday life. He had such a good ear for music. I only had to sing a new song to him once and he could play it.

Going to war irrevocably changes a man but also my father was not the same man after the death of my mother. The sudden, unexpected death of his mother in her mid-sixties only a year later must have been difficult for him to deal with, especially coming so soon after losing his wife.

When I looked after my father in his final illness, I asked him what would be his final message to the present and future generations of his family and he said, *"Love the Lord your God with all your heart, with all your mind and all your strength and your neighbour as yourself."* (Mark 12:30,31)

A 1950'S/EARLY SIXIES CHILDHOOD

The decades after World War II saw a steep rise in the birth rate in the UK. Those born from 1946 to 1964 are known as the baby boomers!

HEALTH

Many aspects of life were very different from today in the 21st century. There was the family doctor (in our case Dr Gimson) who knew all the family and was a consistent figure as we grew up, giving us home visits when we contracted childhood illnesses. When we were young we had orange juice and rosehip syrup from the baby and young children's clinic and in winter, our mother used to give us a regular spoonful of malt and cod liver oil. In our school days, there were periodic inspections from the school nurse.

I remember my mother used to bundle me up with so many layers of clothes in winter. I suppose it was because she grew up in the very cold North East. She would say it doesn't matter what you look like as long as you are warm! I didn't concur with that at the time but I do now. As mentioned earlier, she looked after us very carefully when we were ill.

HOMES

In the 1950s, most homes did not have central heating but relied on coal fires, sometimes supplemented with electric fires to keep warm. I remember the whole family was often engaged in helping my father make paper sticks from tightly rolled up copies of The Daily Telegraph newspaper which provided kindling for the fire. We had a coal fire most of the year which had a back boiler which heated the water. Most people's bedrooms were quite cold in winter. Open fires were generally just in the main living rooms, so we used hot water bottles, thick blankets and eiderdowns or quilts to keep warm. When it was very cold, we would huddle around an electric fire in our parent's bedroom to get dressed in the mornings. We had an open fire in the dining room during the week but at weekends, a fire was lit in the lounge or front room.

Saturday night was bath and hair washing night for the whole family. During the week we would just wash whatever part of us needed washing! When my hair was long, sometimes after washing, my mother would use long strips of rags to wrap around strands of hair and then the strips were tied in a knot. These were taken out the next day and produced "corkscrew" curls called ringlets.

Not many households had washing machines but washed by hand and squeezed out the water with a mangle or in some cases a small spin dryer. White cotton items were often boiled on the hob, especially handkerchiefs. Paper tissues were not in general use until later. Monday, was generally the day when everyone did their washing. I remember my father's shirts were sent to the laundry. Many cotton items had starch sprayed on them before ironing to make them crisper. We tended to wear clothes longer before washing than these days. If an item didn't look soiled and didn't smell it didn't go in the wash.

A few houses, like my maternal grandparent's home, still did not have a bathroom or even an inside toilet, so a tin bath which needed heated water was used for bathing and at night people had "chamber pots" underneath their beds to use during the night instead of venturing out into the cold night to go to the toilet.

Shoe cleaning was a big deal. Our father regularly put black or brown shoe polish on our shoes and gave them a good polish. From what I observed from a child's view, it seemed a disgrace to have scuffed shoes!

Most children didn't have the variety of clothes many children own today. It was common to have school clothes, play clothes and clothes for "best." It was the same for shoes. However, the quality of clothes was often better than today and were made of natural fibres such as wool and cotton. Our shoes were always Clark's shoes which were fitted in the shop according to width (of which there was a choice of several widths) as well as length. We were not allowed to wear second-hand shoes as it was felt it might spoil our growing feet. Later, when we were older, we had great fun painting our shoes and sandals in different colours with Lady Esquire paint.

The Rag and Bone man used to come up our street with his horse and cart shouting loudly what seemed to me to be something

rather unintelligible. According to my mother, he was saying, "Any old iron, any old iron."
Fridges and freezers were also not common. We didn't have one until the 1960s but the larder was quite cold as the wall abutted the garage. As already mentioned, our Richardson grandparents seemed to us to be very modern as they owned one in the 1950s.
Home telephones were also not in widespread use, hence there was an abundance of red phone boxes all around the country! I think it was about two or three old pence to make a call. If you wanted to use one to make a call, you needed to put your money in a slot, dial the number, press button A and when connected, you needed to press button B to be able to hear the other person speak. We were fortunate to have a phone at home. I remember the number was just four digits - 4978 - such a short number due to not many people having a phone. We were on a party line which meant we shared our phone line with someone at the end of our street and if they were having a conversation we could hear them and we had to wait until they had finished before we could phone out or receive calls and vice versa. Consequently, conversations were not private!
Not many people owned a television and the pictures were in black and white. Every time a car went up the road, or my mother used the vacuum cleaner, it would interfere with our television viewing, as there would be a hissing noise and lines would appear over the picture. Television programmes were restricted to certain times of the day. There was nothing in the mornings but at lunchtime, there would be the children's programme *"Watch With Mother"* for pre-school children. *Muffin the Mule, Andy Pandy, Bill and Ben the Flowerpot Men,*

The Woodentops and *Rag, Tag and Bobtail* were programmes that were regularly featured. Later, in the afternoon after older children had returned from school, there was a children's hour featuring programmes such as *Crackerjack*, *Blue Peter* and *Mr. Pastry* and *Billy Bunter*. After this, there would be the 6 o'clock news and more adult programmes. My mother used to have the radio (or the wireless as we called it in those days) during the day and listen to the BBC Home Service. On Saturdays in the late afternoons and early evenings, we would have our tea in the lounge with luscious cakes and watch *Dixon of Dock Green* about a London policeman who was played by Jack Warner. Westerns were a firm favourite with my mother and myself and we watched *The Lone Ranger* and *Laramie*. As mentioned earlier, my mother liked watching Russ Conway playing the piano and I remember her watching Jane Austin's *Emma*. Every evening, the programmes would end with the National Anthem before shutting down for the night. The BBC was the only channel until the 1960s.

GROCERY SHOPPING AND MEALS

There was not the variety of goods we see in the shops these days. For example, I only remember two types of washing powder (no capsules or liquid products) which were Daz and Omo. There was certainly not the array of breakfast cereals we see today. I remember Kelly's Cornflakes and Rice Krispies, Weetabix, Sugar Puffs and Shredded Wheat. Stork is the only margarine I remember. Many people grew their own vegetables and fruit and supermarkets were just coming in so we purchased anything that my mother hadn't grown in the greengrocers. We ate fruit and vegetables in season and my mother bottled fruit and made jam to last us through the winter. On Saturday mornings, I would go with my father to collect a joint of meat from the butcher's shop which my godmother's husband owned. Meat, potatoes and two vegetables were common meals, sometimes with melon or soup for starters. Hot desserts we might have were rice pudding, fruit pies and custard, baked apples with golden syrup and cold desserts like strawberries and cream or fruit salad. Jelly froth was always popular. This was jelly whipped up with evaporated milk.

Pancake Day or Shrove Tuesday were always fun, with my sister and I consuming a large amount of pancakes smothered in lemon and sugar or golden syrup.

Our main meal was at lunchtime when my father would come home from work during his lunch hour. Most children ate their main meal at school in term-time and late afternoon or early evening, we would have a simple meal of Heinz spaghetti or scrambled egg and tomatoes with bread or sometimes fried bread in beef dripping, jam and cake.

In summer, we would sometimes have a salad with ham. Jelly and fruit was a popular dessert and ice-cream when the ice-cream man came in his van to our street as we didn't have a fridge. Sometimes, my mother would send me to get some lemonade and ice-cream from a local shop and we would have ice-cream sodas.

Favourite cakes our mother used to make were "butterfly cakes" (individual sponge cakes with a circle cut out of the top and then the centre was filled with butter icing and the piece of sponge taken out was cut in two and arranged like butterfly wings on top of the cake), meringues, coconut pyramids and Swiss roll. We used to consume rather a large amount of sweets. My father had a sweet tooth and would often bring sweets home when he returned from work and most pocket money went on sweets such as sherbet fountains and liquorice pipes, chocolate bars, gobstoppers, sherbet dib dabs and lemonade or raspberry crystals which we sometimes made into drinks. The local shop used to have quite a lot of large jars filled with various sweets that you could buy even just a couple of ounces worth if you didn't have much money. I used to like lemon sherbets. .

School dinners cost five shillings a week and most of us enjoyed them. They were designed to be nutritious and there would be meals like Shepherd's pie and roast meat and vegetables. The only things I didn't like were the pureed swede and tapioca which we called "frogspawn". We were expected to eat a reasonable amount, otherwise we were kept at the table until we did and missed our playtime. Good table manners were expected and putting our elbows on the table was a ", no, no". Our dinner lady, Mrs. Treadwell who was a little, plump, grandmother type of lady with white hair which she wore in a bun, prowled around the dining room making sure we ate our food and behaved!

The fish man used to come to our street every Friday and the Corona (fizzy drinks) man would visit weekly and if we returned the empty bottles he would give us some money back.

Children were much more active in the 1950s and played outside for much of the time unless the weather was very bad so we burned up the calories from all the food we ate. We were fortunate in having fields at both the top of our road and behind our house.

HOLIDAYS

Apart from going up to the northeast to be with relatives, a favourite place for holidays was Devon and in particular,

Torquay where my parents were married. It was great to go splashing around in the sea and make sandcastles. I remember that when we had picnics on a sandy beach, my father commented that he wasn't too keen on getting sand in his sandwiches! Torquay seemed quite a magical place where the sea was always turquoise in contrast to the usually grey-blue of the sea at home on the southeast coast. The seafront always had coloured lights at night and I remember my mother and I were so excited during one holiday to see an owl in a tree in our hotel garden. One year, we went to some kind of show. I can't actually recall anything about it except a man who wanted a child to come up and sing with him and uncharacteristically for me (as I was usually quite shy), I made my way up onto the stage and joined him. I suppose the fact that I didn't know any of the people there, made it easier as I wouldn't be seeing them again after our holiday if I made a fool of myself!

My mother's cousin also lived in Devon. Cousin Jenny lived with her husband, Billy and their adopted daughter Glenys in Dawlish. A very old gentleman aged over a hundred called Mr Stone also lived with them. Apparently, he was extremely rich and had owned a lot of property in central London and was known as "the Squire of Piccadilly." Jenny, I think had been his housekeeper and Billy, his butler and when they decided to retire to Dawlish, Mr. Stone, having no family went with them. Apparently, I was told that when he died, he did not leave anything to Billy and Jenny, but left everything to their daughter Glenys. Cousin Jenny prided herself on her cooking and looking back, she must have been good to be employed in such an illustrious London house. One summer, we visited them and she had made a loganberry pie. I had never tasted loganberries before but they tasted delicious. However, I was not too keen on pastry, however it was made. Cousin Jenny asked if anyone would like a second helping, to which I replied, "Please could I have the loganberries without the pie." I am not sure how old I was, but I could tell that I had certainly "blotted my copybook" (to use an expression common at that time) as far as she was concerned.

One summer it was decided that we would try a caravan holiday. We went to Bexhill-on-sea and were joined for a day by Auntie Gladys, (my mother's sister), Uncle Ron and our cousins, Michael and Patricia. However, this holiday turned out to be rather eventful! We had a lot of rain and I remember we played the game Beetle quite a lot but the roof sprang a leak and the oven blew up! We never stayed in a caravan again!

Our first holiday out of England was the year my mother died. It was in North Wales and I believe my parents were talking about us going to Austria the following year. Grandpa and Nanna Richardson and Uncle John and Auntie Nellie had already holidayed on the continent. Holidays abroad were just becoming popular with ordinary people rather than the preserve of the rich.

THE GAMES WE PLAYED AND ACTIVITIES WE ENGAGED IN.

Some of the games we played are still played today, but others maybe not. There were a variety of activities and games we engaged in during our breaks at school. In the autumn we would collect the shiny, rich, brown fruit from the horse chestnut trees and engage in games of conkers. I understand it is not played so often these days as it is deemed dangerous! Each person attached their conker to a piece of string and then there were contests to see if you could break your opponent's conker with your superior one. There was always a hunt under horse chestnut trees for the biggest and hardest conkers.

In summer, some of us could be seen (hopefully not by a teacher) burning holes in the school playground tarmac with our magnifying glasses. Hoopla was another popular game and then there were the skipping games.

Skipping games were very popular with us girls. We skipped individually, in pairs and also with a long skipping rope held at each end where several girls would skip together. One such game, we played was where you invited a friend to join you under the same skipping rope saying, "I like coffee, I like tea, I like (name of friend) in with me."

The friend was then asked to leave as the following rhyme was said, "I don't like coffee, I don't like tea, I don't want (friend's name) in with me."

This whole process was repeated with various other friends and then someone else took over from the "main" skipper!

Another game was played with a group. Two children held a long rope at each end and other children joined in skipping while the rope was turned. The following rhyme was chanted

- "Nebuchadnezzar, the king of the Jews, bought his wife a pair of shoes, when the shoes began to wear, Nebuchadnezzar began to swear. When the swearing began to stop Nebuchadnezzar bought a shop" etc. Every time the rhyming word was chanted, the turning of the rope would speed up and the winner of the game was the one who could keep skipping the longest without stopping the rope.

One of the favourite playground games played usually by the girls was when someone stood with their back against a wall and called out different moves for each of the children playing such as, "Take seven giant steps" to which the child mentioned would take seven steps forward extending their legs as far as possible with each step. The next child was asked to take for example twelve fairy steps with each step being only the length of their foot. Then there the "squashed tomato" where a child had to run towards the person by the wall, who would also run towards that child and the child had to stop where they ran into each other. There was also "run to London and back" where a child had to run to the person by the wall (who had their eyes closed) and back until asked to stop. The first child to get to the wall won. Games such as Hide and Seek and Tag (when we chased one another) were popular with both boys and girls. After school, there was a table tennis club at our primary school for the older children which I thoroughly enjoyed.

At home, hopscotch was a game played endlessly with friends in our neighbourhood. We played tennis across the road. It was in the days when there were fewer cars and our road had a cul-de-sac without any through traffic. We enjoyed playing on our bikes, scooters and roller skates. The boys made go-carts out of old prams. Activities such as making models out of plaster of Paris were popular, especially on rainy days. We would pour the plaster into a rubber mould and let it set and then take the item out of the mould and paint it. I seem to remember we did a lot of rabbits!

Snakes and Ladders, Ludo, Bagatelle and Housey Housey were also popular. Housey Housey was a form of Bingo. We enjoyed collecting things such as stamps, coins and coloured glass beads. I remember having a nature club where we would find different flowers and leaves and press them and mount them in a scrapbook. Collecting caterpillars and keeping them in a jar with various leaves for them to eat was popular – poor creatures!

A nice start to the day was when we opened a new cereal packet which invariably in those days had a small toy inside.

It seemed a simpler life with more freedom in those far-off days.

We had great fun putting on "shows" for parents and relatives or just to amuse ourselves with singing and acting. I remember a poem we used to dramatically recite with all the relevant actions which went something like this

I saw a mouse! I saw a mouse! Oh, take me from this dreadful house. I saw it go, beneath the floor. I've never seen a mouse before!

During long summer days, a favourite activity was to make camps in the woods or use a clothes horse, deck chairs and blankets to make a camp in the garden. We would roam the nearby fields and connecting footpaths to a nearby village, have picnics in the field at the top of our road and go to the seaside at Whitstable or Seasalter which was just a few miles from where we lived.

Sometimes, we would go to the Westgate Gardens in

Canterbury. In those days it was like Westgate-on-Sea. There were sand dunes, donkey rides and a boating lake and an outdoor swimming pool.

Autumn was a good time with collecting chestnuts from the woods and roasting them on the fire and there was Bonfire or Guy Fawkes night when we had baked potatoes oozing with butter around a bonfire and fireworks.

During winter, it was always exciting when it snowed and we went tobogganing down a nearby hill in Dukes Meadow.

During the Christmas period, one of the highlights was visiting Lefrevres, the local departmental store in Canterbury. Father Christmas was to be found at the end of a long grotto which featured stories and had moving puppets. Another highlight was a visit to The Marlowe Theatre in Canterbury for The Sidney Woodman ballet school's annual pantomime.

Mr. Cox, our teacher dressed up as Father Christmas at our school Christmas party. He also played his trumpet. This seemed very exciting as he was quite strict in class and was the only teacher who dished out corporal punishment to the girls as well as the boys. If you were talking when you were supposed to be listening to him, he would ask you to put out your hand and would hit your hand a couple of times with a ruler! It stung, but it was bearable. At Christmas we saw a different side to him and despite his strictness, he was actually much loved as he was always very fair and gave the impression that he liked you even when he disciplined you. Teachers and others in authority were much more respected in those days than in some schools now.

The Christmas tree decorations seemed much better quality than those today. The baubles were more substantial. I remember that our Christmas tree lights seemed quite impressive with angels, a Father Christmas, candles etc lit up. It felt particularly exciting when our father brought the Christmas fairy down from the loft to be placed on top of the tree.

Children didn't have as many toys as most of today's children own, so we treasured those we did have and appreciated and got excited about relatively small things, which may not appeal to children in our more sophisticated world.

The Salvation Army came to the bottom of our street and played carols every December.

The Christmas period didn't seem to start until the beginning of December and it certainly wasn't like nowadays when we seem to be bombarded with advertising and Christmas products in the shops as soon as the summer holidays are over.

We always had a Christmas stocking which contained a tangerine and nuts, some shiny coins our mother had polished, a chocolate Father Christmas, sugar mice, a comb set which was sold in aid of blind people and some small toys.

School fetes were always popular events, with many activities such as the coconut shy, hooking ducks and the bran tub. There were stalls with scrummy cakes, sweets and toys.

Sports Day was another highlight. There were running races, hurdles, the high jump, the relay race, the obstacle race, the sack race and the three-legged race. We were put into three teams the Normans who wore a red band across their chest, the Saxons had a green band and the Danes a yellow. Points were awarded to the winners and the team with the most points were the winners for the year and received a cup.

PARTIES

It was always such fun to go to friends' birthday parties where we played many exciting games. There was Kims' game where you had to remember as many items as you could, which were placed on a tray and left there for a few minutes and then taken away.

There was Postman's Knock, This and That (where someone would say, "Do this!" or say, "Do that!" and it was okay if you did what they said when they said, "Do this!" but if you did what they said when they said, "Do that!" then you were out of the game).

Other games were - Hunt the thimble, Put the tail on the Donkey, Musical Chairs, Musical Statues, I went Shopping, where each person, in turn, decided on an item they might buy when shopping and you had to remember the list as each person added to it. Pass the Parcel, In the Manner Of (when you had to mime an activity and do it quickly, stupidly etc and people had to guess the activity and how you performed it) and Charades were also favourite games.

It was fun dressing up for parties. We would wear pretty, pastel-coloured dresses made out of taffeta with a net over the skirt.

MUSIC

My earliest recollection of songs were the usual nursery rhymes that I believe are still sung today. There was *Lavenders Blue, Sing a Song of Sixpence, Humpty Dumpty, Jack and Jill, Three Blind Mice, Ring a ring of Roses, Polly put the Kettle On, The Grand Old Duke of York, Mary, Mary quite Contrary, Little Bo Peep* and many others.

There was also a radio programme of children's songs on Saturday mornings. Some of the songs they played were, *The Billy Goats Gruff, They're Changing Guards at Buckingham Palace,*

The Teddy Bears Picnic, Me and my Teddy Bear, I Love to go a Wandering, Little Brown Jug, The Runaway Train went down the Track and She Blew, Old McDonald Had a Farm and *How much is that Doggie in the Window.*

At home, we used to sing songs from the movies like, *Some Day My Prince will Come* from Snow White and the Seven Dwarfs, *Oh, What a Beautiful Morning* from Oklahoma, songs from South Pacific and songs from Gilbert and Sullivan light operas such as The Mikado. There were also some popular songs like *Que Sera, Magic Moments, Goodbye, Jimmy, Goodbye,* and *Catch a Falling Star and Put It In Your Pocket.*

Our headmaster was very fond of classical music and we would march into assembly with Marche Militaire or the Trumpet Voluntary playing.

In the junior section of our village school, we learned British and Irish folk songs and sea shanties such as *Men of Harlech, Soldier, Soldier, Won't You Marry Me with your Musket Pipe and Drum, Ye Banks and Briars, The Sky Boat song, The Lincolnshire Poacher, What Shall We Do with the Drunken Sailor, Cockles and Mussels, Trelawny* and many others. We also learned to play the recorder at school and at home I had piano lessons.

In my childhood, many children were sent to Sunday school even if their parents didn't go to church very often. I guess that there was a mixture of motives as far as the parents were concerned. They probably thought Sunday School was good for moral training but also enjoyed the peace of some time without their children.

We use to sing such songs as *Wide Wide as the Ocean, Jesus Loves me this I know, I am H-A-P-P-Y, Joy Joy Joy with Joy my Heart is Ringing, In my heart there Rings a Melody* and *Running Over,*

Running Over, my Cups Full and Running Over.
At Brownies and Girl Guides, I remember singing songs such as *Campfire's Burning, The Quartermaster's Stores, Nobody likes me, everybody hates me think I'll go eat worms.*

BROWNIES

I joined the "Brownies" when I was around seven. We had a uniform which consisted of a chocolate brown tunic with a leather belt around our waist and a bright yellow neckerchief/tie. Near the beginning of each session, we would sing the following rhyme -
"We're the Brownies, Here's our aim, Lend a hand and play the game."
We were divided into groups of six and given names such as Sprites, Fairies and Elves. We would dance around a toadstool and begin each session saying, " I promise to do my duty to honour God and the Queen, to help other people at all times and to obey the Brownie law."
I remember my enrolment ceremony. There was also a brownie who was flying up to the Girl Guides. Wings were attached to her and she had to "fly" to the other end of the room to a delegation from the Girl Guides. My mother and sister came to my enrolment. I was so pleased that they were there, but my pleasure turned to embarrassment, as every time I looked at them they obviously thought the whole thing rather funny and they were trying to stifle fits of laughter. Looking back now I can see their point of view. It was a bit ludicrous! Times have changed and I don't think many of today's more sophisticated children would want to participate in such a pantomime, but then perhaps I could be wrong!

MONEY

When I was a child, we had a different kind of currency than today when we have the decimal system. There were 240 pennies to the pound. We also had halfpennies which meant there were 480 units to the pound. Earlier there used to be farthings which were a quarter of a penny bringing the total of 940 units to one pound! An old shilling (or old 12 pence), of which there were 20 to the pound, is now equal to 5 pence in today's money.

I remember that a largish bar of Cadbury's chocolate was 6 pence (two and a half pence in today's money) and my father told me that in the 1920s the same bar of chocolate was only 1 pence.

I was given one shilling and sixpence weekly pocket money for quite a lot of my childhood and I remember that when it was put up to two shillings and sixpence (or half a crown – a crown being five shillings, a quarter of a pound), I felt really rich! Twenty pounds a week was a very good wage in those days and one hundred pounds was regarded as a very large sum of money. One interesting thing that no longer happens was that if you lost some money, you sometimes could get it back at the local police station as it was required by law to hand in any money one found.

Things were certainly quite different in those far-off days. There are pros and cons to everything in life and I have to admit to appreciating modern appliances that make life easier. I also appreciate having central heating, but with some of the advantages of modern technology and changes in society, there has been a price to pay.

Children are brought into the adult world at too young an age.

Availability of junk food, social media and the different society we have these days has had a detrimental effect in terms of physical, emotional and mental health resulting in more loneliness and unhappiness among our young.

A VISIT TO FATHER CHRISTMAS FOR HILARY JANE (FROM A RATHER CRUMPLED OLD PHOTO).

TWO SISTERS.

GRANDMOTHER MARY COMES TO HELP US

After my mother's death, at mealtimes, my father, older sister and I sat at the dining room table which had four chairs. My mother's empty chair emphasized her absence.

My father's mother, our grandmother Mary came down south from Sunderland and spent time living with us and helping us over the next year. She didn't make up for my mother's absence but it did help. She adored us all! I remember my father feeling that she was spoiling me. He said to her, "Mam, either I give her pocket money or you do. It's not good that she gets so much money!"

I remember her singing one of her favourite hymns as she did the house work. I can still hear her voice singing it in my head as I write this.

Jesus keep me near the cross. The chorus goes – In the cross, in the cross, be my glory ever, till my ransomed soul shall find rest beyond the river. I never expected her to find that rest so soon.

She died suddenly of a heart attack just one year and two days after my mother. Now, the two people in the world who were most demonstrative in their love for us were gone. I was eleven years old and felt very alone inside but life had to go on.

About fifteen months after our grandmother's death, my father felt it was unfair for my sister to have to run the house, so a relative of a friend came to do housekeeping for us. My father married her a few months later.

14

MY SPIRITUAL JOURNEY

As a young teenager, I ran away from home to some family friends. The husband was the man who collected me from school the day my mother died and the family belonged to our church. They had known me since I was small.

That night I went to bed and had a very interesting experience. There had been big changes in our church and some people had experienced being "baptised in the Holy Spirit" and speaking in new languages as in the Books of Acts and the apostle Paul's writings in the Bible. I was very intrigued by all this so prayed that I would have this experience, as I had many doubts about Christianity and I felt this would help me believe.

You don't need to have this experience to know that you are a Christian, it's just how I felt in my youthful way at that time. In the middle of the night, I woke up and found myself muttering a few words in another language. I was half asleep and went back to sleep very quickly. I awoke the next morning and my first thought was, "What was that in the middle of the night?" I opened my mouth to speak and all that would come out was this new language. My next thought was, "How can God bless me in this way when I have run away from home?" I reached out for my Bible and asked God to lead me to a particular scripture. I opened it up and put my finger on the page. The words were from Psalm 66 -

I cried to the Lord with my mouth, and He was extolled with my tongue. If I regard iniquity in my heart the Lord will not hear me but certainly God has heard me and He has attended to the voice of my prayer. Blessed be God Who has not turned away from my prayer, nor withheld His mercy from me.

The experience of speaking in tongues is recorded in the Bible in the book of Acts.

John the Baptist said that Jesus would baptise in the Holy Spirit. (Matthew 3:11 Mark 18 Luke 3:16 John 1:33.)

Jesus also said that he would baptise in the Holy Spirit. (Act 1 15.)

In Acts 2 when the Holy Spirit came upon 120 people they spoke in languages they had never learnt which was understood by the many Jewish foreigners who were visiting Jerusalem at that time. In other parts of Acts and in the writings of the Apostle Paul there are references to people speaking in known languages of men and also angelic languages, in which case God would give a gift of interpretation.

THE REV. ALEXANDER BODDY AND SUNDERLAND'S CHRISTIAN HERITAGE

Interestingly, although there have been records of people speaking in tongues over the centuries since the early church, it was in Sunderland in 1907 that the teaching and experience of being baptised in the Holy Spirit started to become more widespread. Rev Alexander Boddy was Vicar of All Saints Monkwearmouth in Sunderland and God used him to start a movement where these biblical truths eventually would be brought back into mainstream Christianity.

It is mainly these churches that have grown phenomenally around the world today. Many people view speaking in tongues as a rather emotional experience, which was certainly not the case with me when I first spoke in tongues as I was half asleep!

The person speaking in tongues can choose to speak either loudly or softly! A television programme that investigated speaking in tongues, interestingly found the part of the brain associated with speech is actually dormant. Speaking in tongues come from a person's spirit, directed by the Holy Spirit, so you don't have to think about what you say as with normal speech. Sunderland has had a reputation for being a very spiritual place for many centuries. It was the birthplace of the Saxon scholar The Venerable Bede who as mentioned earlier, was considered to be the most learned Englishman of his age. Geoffrey Milburn, a local church historian commented that even in the 1600s, there was "an outspokeness and tolerance due to being a seaport" among the people of Sunderland so the events with Alexander Boddy in Monkwearmouth were more likely to take place there than in places where people had more closed minds. John Wesley was the founder of the Methodist Church, although he never intended it to be separate from the Anglican church. He travelled the length and breadth of Britain often doing 4 - 5000 miles a year over rough terrains bringing a strong Christian message of morality and hope which resulted in many changed lives, particularly among the poorer of society. Some historians credit him with saving Britain from something like the French Revolution which was happening in France at that time.

John Wesley visited Sunderland more than thirty times from 1743 to 1790, preaching in St. Peter's Monkwearmouth at least fifteen times. He wrote in 1752, "I rode to Sunderland where I found one of the liveliest societies in the North of England". His brother, Charles on preaching in Sunderland for the first time commented in his journal, "Never have I seen greater attention in any at their first hearing.

LEAVING HOME AND MEETING MY FUTURE HUSBAND

I really wanted to leave home as soon as possible and found out that it was possible to do a 2-year nursery nursing course that would offer accommodation in London so at just a week after my sixteenth birthday, I set off for London. My father and stepmother were fostering a Polish girl at the time. Christine had previously been with my sister and brother-in-law who now had emigrated to Australia.

She came up to London to stay with me one weekend but when it was time for her to go home, after boarding the underground train, she told me that she had decided not to go back to Canterbury but stay in London. I was dismayed! I knew my father was going to meet Christine off the train in Canterbury and that he would not be a happy man if she did not appear. I prayed silently. The train was packed and we had to stand. I glanced down and noticed a guy sitting with a pile of books on his lap. I casually looked at the titles and realised they were Christian books and as I read the last title I was aware that he was looking up at me.

I said, "Oh, you're a Christian!" whereupon he leapt up out of his seat, books going everywhere and shook my hand enthusiastically saying how wonderful it was that I wasn't ashamed to mention Christianity in public. (Which I thought was rather a strange comment to make!) However, he turned out to be the answer to my prayer. His name was Henry and he even spoke Polish. He was a Polish Jew so he spoke to Christine in Polish, persuaded her to go home and travelled to Victoria station with us.

After she had gone, Henry turned to me and said, "I think you should go with Operation Mobilisation this summer". I had heard about this organisation but didn't know much about them apart from an impression that they were a group of enthusiastic young people who told people about Christianity. Henry was staying at the Chinese church in London and invited me for a meal to discuss O.M. the shortened version of Operation Mobilisation. I decided to go to Europe and work with a young people's team with O.M. so I went to Belgium for the week-long training conference and to France for three weeks. It was there I was to meet my future husband! I met Dick that summer and rather liked him, but he continued with O.M. going off to work in India and I still had my course to finish. We exchanged letters over the next year which he also did with several other girls.

As mentioned earlier, I went to live in the Northeast. After some time, my grandfather Richardson introduced me to one of his neighbours and as the memory of Dick was fading and I didn't know if anything would come of our relationship, I started going out with Paul and it looked as if my plan to make the Northeast my permanent home would come about.

However, after some time, I heard from Dick that he was coming back to England to study for his marine engineer's seconds ticket so he could work on the ship O.M. was buying. He had previously got a second engineer's ticket for steam ships, but O.M. was going to buy a motor vessel.

I suddenly felt that I needed to find out if there was any future for Dick and I, so I told Paul about him. Things were not working out so well with Paul due to his very possessive mother. She had ruined every relationship he'd had. He was her only son and Paul's father was much older than her and not well.

I told Paul that I needed to go to Birmingham where Dick

was living. Paul dropped me off at the main bus station in Sunderland and said that he would wait five minutes to see if I got on the bus. We both agreed that if I did, it would be the end of our relationship. I got to the coach just in time to see it leave, but on going to where Paul's car had been, I saw that he had gone and so it was, I did go to Birmingham and my life took a different direction.

RICHARD AND HILARY (NEE RICHARDSON) WYATT.

MARRIAGE, LIVING ABOARD A SHIP AND BABIES.

Not long after Dick arrived back from India, Eldin Corsie, a minister of the church I had attended whilst in London married us in Carlisle where my father and stepmother were now living. We went back with O.M. first spending a few months in France and then with O.M.'s new ship MV Logos. During this period our daughter Nicola was born in Cochin, South India followed by the birth of our son Andrew when we arrived back in England.

CANTERBURY CHRISTIAN FAMILY CONFERENCE

Continuing the story of my spiritual journey, it had been quite some time since that night when God gave me a new language with which to praise Him. It had made a big difference in my life but sometimes I felt there was something missing.

At that time we often used to go and camp at a Christian conference that was held annually in Canterbury. One particular year, Roger Forster from Ichthus Christian Fellowship preached on the Lordship of Jesus Christ. As he preached, I suddenly realised that I enjoyed being a Christian but a lot of the time I made my own decisions without consulting God. When I was younger, I was told about Revelation 3:20 where Jesus comes and knocks at the door of our hearts and we were encouraged to ask Jesus into our hearts, but it had only just occurred to me that the heart is the seat of all our desires and asking Jesus into my heart meant giving all of my life to him.

I knew that this was something I needed to do and so right there in the meeting, I silently told Jesus that I wanted Him to have all of my life. It is so easy to think we are in charge of our own destinies but in a moment everything we hold dear can be taken away from us, for there is nothing enduring on this earth. Sometimes we can think we know best as we make decisions in our lives but in fact, everything works better when it is done according to the Maker's instructions and our Heavenly Father wants the best for us and to save us from some of the disastrous mistakes we could make without Him.

As I made this decision to let Jesus be in charge of my life, a feeling of joy welled up inside me. The meeting was drawing to a close and it was suggested that people could remain to pray in groups or leave quietly and go back to their tents. Immediately,

I suggested to friends around me that we stay and pray.
They readily agreed and we sat in a circle. I felt happy and was looking forward to having a time of praise and worshipping God together. My thoughts were interrupted by a friend we called Auntie Audrey who was sitting on my left. She said to me, "Hilary, I have a feeling that you need to give your mother back to God!" All eyes were on me. This was not what I wanted and I felt uncomfortable.

The next moment I was aware of a surge of anger rising up inside me. It surprised me as I didn't regard myself as an angry person. I covered it up and answered in a level tone, "I don't know what you mean. I'm sure I have come to terms with her death. It is now quite a long time ago and when I do think of her, I think of happy past memories."

Auntie Audrey replied that despite what I had just said, she still felt I needed to give my mother back to God and asked me gently if I could try and say the words, "Heavenly Father, I give my mother to you." As she was speaking, I realised I had a problem and that she was right.

I tried to get the words out but it was as if something was gagging me. I thought back to my earlier decision to let Jesus be the Lord of my life and realised that this was my first test. I realised that something within me did not want to say these words, but I knew that I needed to say them.

I suddenly understood that inside I was angry that my mother had gone. I managed to get out the word God and then I heard a sound of loud horrible wailing that resounded all over the marquee and realised to my horror and embarrassment that it was me as grief and pain that have been pushed down for years came out.

I went back to our tent and into the "bedroom" that I normally shared with Dick who was working on the cross-channel ferries that night. The song that we had been singing earlier was going through my head, *"Jesus, Jesus, Jesus, Your love has melted my heart,"* when I was totally enveloped in a bright light that shut everything else out and I felt Jesus pouring His love all over me, wave after wave after wave.

It seemed as if I spent the whole night in this state. When I came to and it was morning, I felt saturated both inside and out with the presence and love of God.

15

CAN IT REALLY BE TRUE?

Growing up I really wanted to know for myself if Christianity could really be true. I had always had questions about life as long as I can remember. One of my earliest memories when I was probably around three years old, was of walking down our long garden, feeling my hands and thinking how odd it was that I was here! I remember going to the beach and staring at all the pebbles and thinking that I was just like a pebble, so insignificant among all the people living, those who'd gone before us and those who would come after us.

As far as Christianity was concerned, I really did not just want to follow something because I had been told it was a good idea. As I studied the subject there were some things that helped me in my quest.

First of all, there were the supernatural experiences which I have mentioned earlier and there has been other miracles and manifestation of God's presence that I have witnessed over the years. Secondly, after much study and some life experience, I have found that the Bible has answered many of my questions. I wouldn't be so presumptuous to claim to have all the answers but over the years I have observed that when someone loses their faith, something very precious at the core if their being has left them. We are made up of body, soul and spirit and that spiritual part of them has been obscured.

I invite my readers to have an open mind as I share some of my findings with you. The Bible can be a difficult book to understand and indeed, it cannot really be understood without divine help.

It actually consists of a collection of books written by as many as forty different authors over more than 1600 years. There are parts that are historical, poetic, prophetic and allegorical and although the background of the people who wrote it needs to be taken into account, its message is timeless. The Old Testament or the Old Covenant which comprises a huge part of the Bible is the New Testament or New Covenant concealed and the New Testament or Covenant is the Old Covenant or Old Testament revealed. The Old Testament actually points to the coming of Jesus in many ways.

Sometimes the Bible can appear to contradict itself but it is like a coin with two pictures on each side but it is the same coin. Apart from eyewitness accounts found in the New Testament of Jesus's life, birth, death and subsequent resurrection and the eminent and respected 1st century historian Josephus writing about him, there are numerous prophecies concerning Jesus in the Old Testament. These prophecies were written many centuries before Jesus' birth.

They foretold the circumstances of his birth, where he was to be born, His ancestry, that he would be born to a virgin, details of his life and the manner and circumstances surrounding his death and that he would rise from the dead. Scholar Alfred Edershein concluded that there are at least 456 passages in the Old Testament that Jewish rabbis historically have interpreted about the Messiah. Others have said there are over 300.

The odds of anyone fulfilling this amount of prophecies is staggering. Mathematicians put it this way: 1 person fulfilling 8 prophecies – 1 in 100,000,000,000,000,000 (10 to the power of 17), 1 person fulfilling 48 prophecies – 1 chance in 10 to the power of 157, 1 person fulfilling 300 prophecies – ONLY JESUS!

Everything in nature points to there being a Creator. It is interesting that in modern times some scientists who are not religious are saying that after careful examination, everything in nature points to there being a creator. For some that has led them on a journey of faith. Here are just a few of their observations –

The astronomer Fred Doyle, as he reflected on the energy needed to produce large quantities of carbon, wrote the following, "Some super calculating intellect must have designed the properties of the carbon atom, otherwise the chance of finding such an atom through the blind forces of nature would be utterly minuscule – a super-intellect has monkeyed with physics, and with the chemistry and biology. The numbers one calculates from the facts seemed to me so overwhelming as to put this conclusion almost beyond question.

A very small change of nuclear resonance by 1 or 2% and there would be no carbon and hence no carbon-based life such as ours. (Fred Hoyle, *The Universe: Past and Present – Reflections in Engineering and Science*. Nov.1981 pp. 8-12)

There are many examples of the physical laws being fine-tuned for life: if the force of gravity and electromagnetism, as well as the mass of sub-atomic particles, were ever so slightly different, life on Earth would be impossible. If the expansion of the universe had been more even, stars and planets would not have been formed. If the forces in the atomic nuclei were weaker, the universe would be made of hydrogen; if stronger, then oxygen would be the base element. If the strengths of the strong nuclear force were changed by a small figure such as 0.5% then life on earth would be impossible. (John Marsh - author of *The Liberal Delusion*)

The philosopher, Anthony Flew used to be one of Britain's leading atheists, but by 2004 two scientific discoveries changed his mind. First, The Big Bang Theory showed the universe began at a particular point in time. This raises the question, what caused the universe to begin? Secondly, the universe appears to have been fine-tuned for life. Flew wrote, "Not merely are there regularities in nature, but they are mathematically precise, universal and tied together. How did nature come packaged in this fashion? Scientists from Newton to Einstein to Heisenberg have answered the Mind of God." (Anthony Flew, *There is a God*. London Harper One page 96 2007)

Discover magazine suggests that there are around 700 quintillion (7 followed by 20 zeros) planets in the universe, but only one like earth. Astrophysicist Eric Zackrisson said that one of the requirements for a planet to sustain life is to orbit in the "Goldilocks zone", where the temperature is just right and water can exist. Out of the 700 quintillion planets, Earth seems to be planet where conditions are just right.

Finally, Jesus' disciples were so afraid of the Jewish leaders that they all fled when Jesus was arrested except Peter who denied knowing Jesus three times. After Jesus was crucified they stayed behind locked doors as they were so frightened. However, later all these men were martyred and suffered horrible deaths for their faith in Jesus except John who was exiled. Would these men who at one time were so frightened of dying have laid down their lives for something that wasn't true? What changed these men? It was that they had seen the risen Christ!

Nothing on this earth is forever. The truth is that none of us is really in charge of our own destiny. Everything we can see and touch is subject to deterioration, some things at a quicker rate than others. The Bible says our bodies were formed from the dust of the ground. The same essential chemical elements are found in man and animal life that are in the soil. This scientific fact was not known until relatively recent times.

We think things are real because we can experience them with our senses yet who is to say that some of the things we can't see aren't more real than the things we can see? Some of us may find it difficult to believe in what we do not see. However, we can believe in electricity which we can't see. We believe in it because we can see its power when we plug in our electrical appliances. If we want to believe in spiritual things we cannot understand them with our human senses but as we "plug" into God, we will begin to see the results of his power. How do we plug into God? The Bible says that the only way to God is through Jesus. He said, "I am the way, the truth and the life, no one comes to the Father except through me." The Bible says that "God so greatly loved the world that he sent his son that whoever believes in him will live forever." (Amplified Bible John 3:16)

Things always work best when done according to the makers instructions. We were never designed to know evil and it's consequences, the ultimate consequence being death. It is interesting that many doctors subscribe to the view that at least three quarters of sickness has its roots in negative emotions such as anger, hatred, fear, loneliness and grief - all results of when Man decided to put his wisdom above God's, our Heavenly Father. We were designed to be in an unbroken, intimate, loving relationship with our Creator.

God, your Heavenly Father loves you and wants the best for you and things always work out best when they are done according to his plan for you.

The Bible refers to God as the perfect Father. (Matthew 5:48). Paul, the apostle wrote, "I (Paul) bow my knees before the Father of my Lord Jesus Christ, for whom every family in heaven and on earth is made (that Father from whom all fatherhood takes its title and derives its name)" (Ephesians 3:14-15 Amplified Bible).

Fathers are so important – as are mothers of course! A good father gives us a sense of belonging and worth. He is a good role model for his sons and affirms them as they grow into manhood so that they will have he confidence and the ability to raise their families. He affirms his daughters as they grow into womanhood and how they relate to men will be influenced by their relationship with their father. It is interesting to watch little children growing up and observe that girls as well as boys have an inbuilt desire to have a father figure to look up to! It is a sad fact these days, that by the time they are fifteen only about half of our children still have their father living with them.

The Bible says that God is love and He is the perfect parent. In the Greek New Testament, there are two particular words for love. One of them is *agape* and the other is *phileo*.

Agape type of love has been defined as a love that seeks the best for others, a sacrificial love, a love formulated in the mind that starts with an act of the will, causing a decision to be made to be committed to another person, no matter what happens.

Phileo type of love has been defined as having an affection, passion or feeling for another, a fondness based in the heart. Phileo love is about **feelings or emotions**. Both these

Greek words are attributed to God in the Bible and are key to understanding how he parents us.

Without the phileo type of love, we might feel that our Heavenly Father was a hard father. Children find it difficult to be told that something is being done "for their own good" when a parents shows little or no warmth towards them. Without the agape type of love, we would not know that commitment God has for us as a Father who never changes, always wants the best for us and will never let us down. Our love is like a bartering system which manifests itself as, "I'll love you and be nice to you if you love me and be nice to me - but if you are horrible to me, I won't love you anymore." God loves us even if we reject him. He gives us free will but the wonderful thing is that as we come to him and let him parent us, he will begin the work of healing us from the hurts and deficits of the past.

Much is made these days of "being whatever you want to be," but the truth is that we can only find our true identity from our Maker.

Whatever has happened in your life, whatever abuse or traumas you may have suffered, whatever mistakes or wrong decisions you have made, your Heavenly Father wants to heal your pain. If you have not already done so, will you make that decision to put your faith in Jesus? Tell him you are sorry for living your life your way and give your life to him. The following is a suggested prayer you might like to use or you could use your own words-

Jesus, I am sorry for living my life my way. I now give you my life. Please forgive me for all my past mistakes and heal me of past hurt. I thank you that you loved me so much that you died on the cross for me and conquered the power of death so that I can live with you forever. I receive you right now as my Lord and Saviour.

"She (Mary) will bear a Son and you shall call his name Jesus (the Greek form of the Hebrew, Joshua which means Saviour) for he will save his people from their sins, that is prevent them from failing and missing the true end and scope of life which is God." (Amplified Bible Matthew 1: 27).

For more information see *Finding Real Freedom* by Hilary Wyatt (yet to be published)

16

WHAT IF?

As I have mentioned earlier, sometimes we can think we are in charge of our own destiny but so much of our lives have been affected by the decisions of previous generations.
What if, the De Henzells and Tyzacks had not come from their native Bohemia? What if they had been murdered in the St. Bartholomew's massacre? What if they had not chosen to leave Alsace Lorraine to settle in Newcastle-upon-Tyne? The families on my father's side would not exist!
What if James Saunders hadn't gone to live in Seaham Harbour, hundreds of miles from his roots?
What if my grandfather Ernest Saunders had settled in the States with his family? The families on my mother's side would not exist!
What if my father's plane had been shot down along with the five or six Lancasters he saw go down after the Stettin raid or he hadn't developed M.S. and had been shot down later with the rest of his crew?
What if my father and mother hadn't decided to settle in South East England, hundreds of miles from their roots? My sister's and my family would not exist!
What if I had not met Henry on a London tube and ended up meeting my husband in France?
If Billy Graham had not come to England and my parents had not decided to embrace Christianity, I would probably not have gone for the summer with O.M. The founder of O.M. (which now works in over 100 countries and has had 5 ships over the

years) George Verwer became a Christian after hearing Billy Graham preach, so also, if that hadn't happened, O.M. would not exist and I wouldn't have met my husband so without Billy Graham, our children and grandchildren would not exist!

It is interesting that when James Saunders from my mother's side of the family, came to Seaham Harbour, he lodged with a couple whose surname was Merchant which was the surname of my father's mother.

I have two lovely brothers from my father's second marriage, Paul and John. Paul has three sons, Joseph, Samuel and Edward and John has sons, Ben and Leo and daughter, Sophie.

In recent years, 1 was having a phone conversation with the daughter of my grandfather, George Henry Winship Richardson's cousin, whom I connected with through a family history site. She had previously spoken of her son and grandchildren living in a village near Cambridge. On this occasion, I asked her where in Cambridgeshire, they lived. She replied that they lived in a village called Linton. "Wow!" I said, "My brother Paul and his family live there!" It turned out that Paul's children and Margaret's grandchildren all went to school together and knew each other. They obviously didn't know that they shared family lines. As it has been said, "It's a small world!"

17

TINKER, TAILOR, SOLDIER, SAILOR

I remember when my mother, Dereen first told me about her father's grandparents, James and Dorothy. It was one lunchtime and she was using binoculars to have a look at a jay who was feeding in our garden.

I was finishing off my dessert which must have been something like plums which contained stones. A silly little game which some children played in those days went like this – over the stones, I said, "Who am I going to marry?" and proceeded to say the following words over each stone – "Tinker, tailor, soldier, sailor, rich man, poor man, beggar man, thief."

My mother looked over at me and told me that the binoculars she was using belonged to James Saunders who used them in the 1880s when he was at sea. She said that maybe I would marry someone who went to sea like James and that, maybe I would grow up to be some kind of nurse like his wife Dorothy.

My mother never did see me grow up but I did become a nursery/maternity nurse. I did marry a marine engineer, and we both went to sea and so did our daughter Nicola, born in Cochin India while we were serving on the ship M.V. Logos and, where later on the same ship, I became pregnant with our son, Andrew.

MV LOGOS

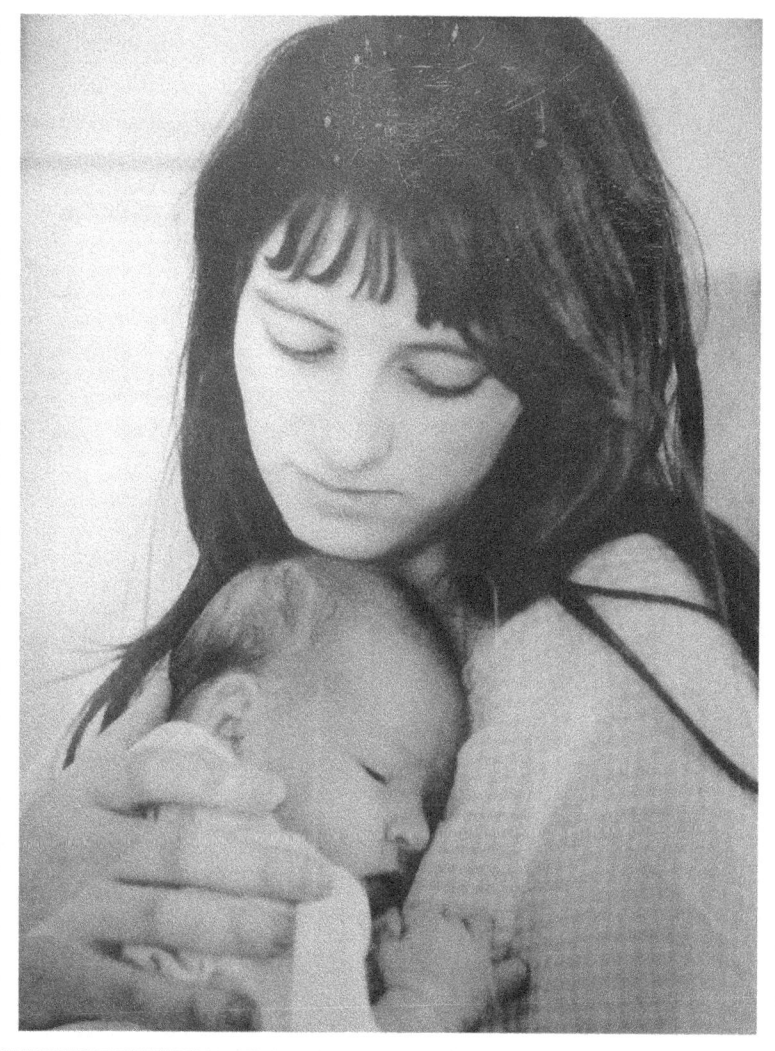

NICOLA, ONE DAY OLD IN COCHIN INDIA

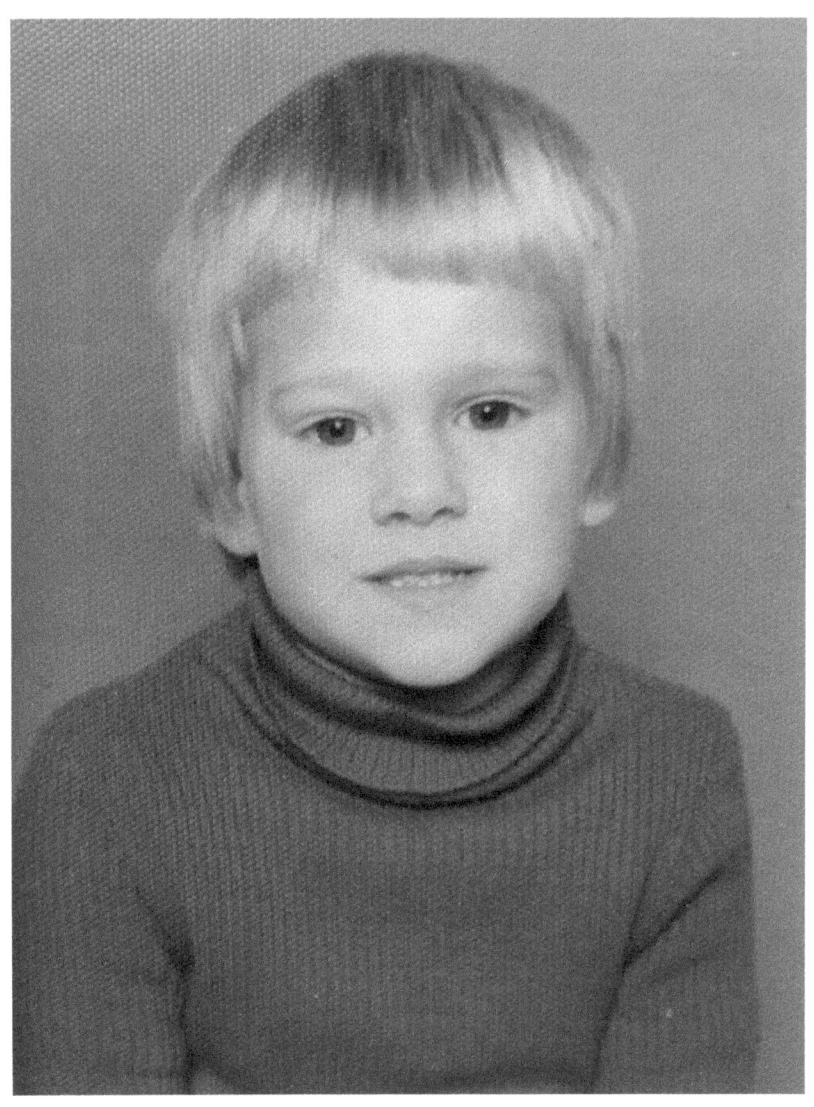

ANDREW

NICOLA, ONE DAY OLD IN COCHIN INDIA

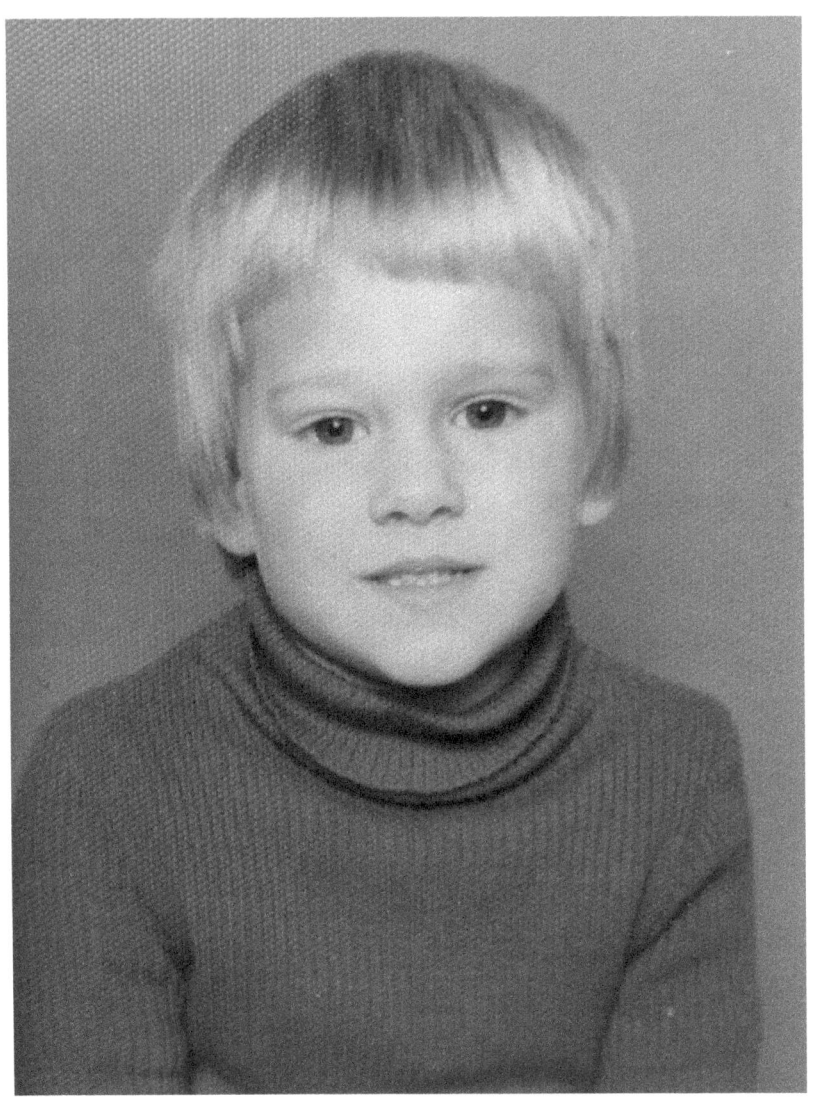

ANDREW

APPENDIX AND BIBLIOGRAPHY

CHAPTER 1 THE OCEAN QUEEN
Information taken from the booklet - *Good Men Remembered The Disaster of The Eliza Adams* Friday, October 29th 1880. 125 years – A Commemoration.

CHAPTER 2 A SMALL HAMLET BECOMES A THRIVING TOWN
The Hole in the Wall by Fred Cooper.

CHAPTER 3 JAMES AND DOROTHY IN SEAHAM HARBOUR
www.kidcyber.com.au7gold-rush
Information was taken from a letter by Rev. Alexander Boddy regarding the miner's strike to The Times newspaper appealing for help. 18th April 1892.
Sunderland The Biggest Shipbuilding Town in the World by Alan Brett and Andrew Clark
SUNDERLAND Pictorial Record of Wearside Published by The Sunderland Echo 1948
HARRY WATTS Information regarding Harry Watts obtained from Sunderland Museum Mowbray Park Sunderland

CHAPTER 4 SEAHAM HARBOUR AT THE TURN OF THE 20TH CENTURY
The Hole in the Wall by Fred Cooper.
On The Banks of the Wear by Alan Brett published by Black Cat Publications

CHAPTER 6 THE HUGUENOTS

Cassels Book of Knowledge
Desbois's Dictionary
Website – Geneanet by Phillip Adenbrooke
Foxes Book of Martyrs by John Foxe Foxes Book of Martyrs was written by John Foxe. He was born in Lincolnshire in 1516 and died on April 18th 1587. His very well-researched book has some information obtained by those who had known those who were martyred and some who had witnessed the martyrdoms. The Huguenot massacre occurred during Foxe's lifetime.

CHAPTER 8 ERNEST AND RACHEL

Shaftesbury - The Reformer Biography by John Pollock. Published by Kingsway.

CHAPTER 10 GEORGE AND DEREEN AND THE 2ND WORLD WAR

The Turrets of War Douglas Eades Janus Publishing Company. SUNDERLAND Pictorial Record of Wearside. The Sunderland Echo 1948

CHAPTER 12 MEMORIES OF THE NORTHEAST AND RELATIVES

Information regarding housing taken from – *Sunderland The Biggest Shipbuilding Town in the World* by Alan Brett and Andrew Clark

CHAPTER 13 HOPE AND HEARTACHE
The BILLY GRAHAM Story by John Pollock Published by Zondervan
Comments regarding Queen Elizabeth's last days - Catherine Pepinster Author of *Defenders of the Faith – the British Monarchy, Religion and the Coronation.*

CHAPTER 14 MY SPIRITUAL JOURNEY
Grace and Love Like Mighty Rivers Hilary Wyatt Published by Verite.
Alexander Boddy, Pentecostal Pioneer by Gavin Wakefield published by Paternoster

CHAPTER 15 CAN IT REALLY BE TRUE?
The Amplified Bible
We Will Dance on the Streets that are Golden by Hilary Wyatt published by New Wine
Source of information from Discover Magazine – Marvin Williams *Our Daily Bread* Publications.

Also thanks go to Genes Reunited, Durham and Northumberland records and Fred Cooper.

APPENDIX AND NOTES

CHAPTER 14 - WHAT IS THE PURPOSE OF SPEAKING IN TONGUES?

The following is an extract taken from the book – *I Thank God That I Speak In Tongues More Than You All* by Hilary Wyatt published by New Wine.

The title of this book is taken from a quote by the Apostle Paul in the Bible.

Since the early church, the practice of speaking in tongues has continued to some degree over the centuries, but it was the events in 1907 at All Saints Church Monkwearmouth, Sunderland whose vicar was Alexander Boddy (mentioned in chapter 14) that began a movement which caused the use of tongues to begin to become more widespread in Britain.

The practice of speaking in tongues is first recorded in the Bible when John the Baptist's prediction came to pass at Pentecost that Jesus would baptise his disciples with the Holy Spirit and with fire. Jesus said to his disciples when he was speaking of sending the Holy Spirit "He lives with you and will be in you". John 14:17 New King James Version.

John the Baptist stated that he baptised with water but Jesus was the one who would come to baptise with the Holy Spirit and with fire. John the Baptist was likened in the Bible to a type of Elijah. At Mount Carmel Elijah had soaked the sacrifice with water three times (Jesus spoke about baptising in the Name of the Father, Son and Holy Spirit), but he couldn't provide the fire (1 Kings 18: 16-46). The sacrifice was sufficiently soaked for there to be no doubt of any sort of spontaneous combustion happening. There needed to be a Supernatural act of God to bring the fire to burn up the sacrifice. John the Baptist like Elijah could baptise with water but it took the Son of God, Jesus to baptise with fire! (Matthew 3:11 Luke 3:16.)

As Elijah selected the 12 stones to represent the nation of Israel (which had 12 tribes), we can become part of God's people. As the water "baptised" those stones and the supernatural fire of God even burned them up, we can be as it were "crucified with Christ" and (as the Bible says), we can partake of his baptism, then the Holy Spirit of God will bring the fire to consume the sacrifice of our natural life and make us holy and righteous before God so we can also be resurrected with Christ.

The Apostle Paul wrote about speaking in tongues and said that they were tongues of men and also angelic tongues. However, what is the use of speaking in tongues? First of all, as at Pentecost, we can use them to praise God.

It is important to realise that the language or languages that the Holy Spirit can give us comes through our spirit and not through our minds or emotions although you can feel emotional when speaking in tongues just as you can when speaking in your mother tongue. When I first spoke in tongues I woke up in the middle of the night and that had a few words in tongues before going back to sleep I certainly didn't feel emotional just sleepy! When someone investigated speaking in tongues for a television programme they found that the part of the brain that formulates the speech was dormant. This was only confirming what had been written in the Bible by the Apostle Paul! 1 Corinthians 14:14.

The Apostle Paul also said that speaking in tongues was a sign to those who don't yet know Jesus. Examples of this are as follows - A van load of us from Operation Mobilisation went down to Weston-Super-Mare to a Worship and the Arts conference. After the first session, my friend and I noticed two of our guys were engaged in a discussion with a young man who appeared to have walked in off the street. They talked for a while but felt it was rather a fruitless conversation. My friend reckoned that he was probably on drugs and that she could see it in his eyes as well as the way he conversed.   During the remainder of the conference we saw this young man several times in the foyer but seeing him talking again with our guys after the final session of the conference I felt God say to me that I should pray with him before he left. I looked at the book table while keeping an eye out for him. Eventually, he made for the exit door. I quickly went to him and asked if I could pray with him. He shrugged his shoulders and said, "Ok!" I gently put my hand on his shoulder and started to pray a prayer that I always use when praying for someone who is sceptical where I basically align myself with them and say, "Father God please reveal to us your truth." As I was saying this I felt God telling me to pray for him in tongues. I felt a resistance inside me. I have never prayed in tongues with someone who doesn't believe in Christianity. Would he think that I was mad? I felt the Holy Spirit again telling me to go ahead so with my hands still on this young man's shoulder, I closed my eyes and tried to block out my surroundings and feelings of apprehension. I began to pray very quietly in tongues close to his ear. I hadn't been praying long before I felt God's presence very strongly. I said to God silently "What is this! This is not so I feel blessed but it is for this young man." What happens if, at the end of this, he thinks that I'm mad? After I had finished praying in tongues I opened my eyes and looked at the young man. He was staring at me with a puzzled expression on his face. "What was that?" He asked. I thought to myself Oh no! He does think I am mad! I replied that after praying for him in English I then prayed for him in a language that God gave me. I went on to explain further from the Book of Acts. It was quite amazing because God gave me all the words, as I finished one phrase, he gave me the next and so on until I was finished. The whole thing was explained in a way that was better than anything I could have done. I noticed that the young man was listening intensely and when I had finished, he exclaimed, "I feel so good! I feel so good!" and then he was receptive to the good news of Jesus.

Since that occasion I have experienced the prompting of the Holy Spirit to pray in tongues with those who do not know Jesus on quite a number of occasions such as the time when a young man was writhing in pain after a motorbike accident and an old lady had a fall in the middle of the town and on being prayed for in tongues following a prayer in English the pain instantly left them.

Not long after the weekend in Weston-super-Mare, a few of us from Operation Mobilisation went to an evening meeting at the Emmanuel Centre in central London. It had been quite a warm day but as we came out of the meeting it was certainly on the chilly side. We walked along Victoria Street towards Victoria Station hoping to catch a taxi but none passed us.

As we walked along we saw a man lying on the pavement with another man trying to get him up. We went round them and walked on. I was the last person to do so but wondering what was going on, I found myself looking back. My eyes looked at the man on the ground and in that moment I felt an overwhelming love for him which I recognised was God's love for him. I hardly knew how I got there but the next thing, I was on the ground next to him. My first thought was that the others would not be impressed with me as everyone was so cold. I found myself saying to the man "Do you know God loves you?" I looked at his eyes which were rolling. It was obvious that he was drunk or under the influence of drugs. I felt at a total loss as to what to do! I then got very near to him and said into his ear, "What's your name?" and got a strange noise back. At last, it dawned on me that he was in no fit state for communication so I decided to pray for him. After I had finished and there was no perceptible change in the man I felt God tell me to pray for him in tongues so I started quietly to speak in tongues close to his ear and after a little while I became aware of the others who were with me also praying in tongues. I looked into the man's eyes and realised something miraculous was taking place and found myself taking his hands and gently lifting him to his feet, we talked to him about Jesus and his coordination was restored to him and his speech was perfectly clear. Afterwards, I felt God say to me that when we pray in tongues under the direction of the Holy Spirit, it doesn't matter if the person is unconscious or under the influence of something, His Holy Spirit can reach their spirit.

CHAPTER 13 HOPE AND HEARTACHE - WHEN IT'S TIME TO SAY GOODBYE

It is an indisputable fact that nothing we have on this earth is forever. Days come when we have no choice but to say goodbye to those we love. It has been said that "Grief is the price we pay for loving", but another saying is also true: "It is better to have

loved and lost than never to have loved at all."
Some of us face parting from a loved one when we are young. As recounted in chapter 13, I was 10 years old when I came home from school to find that my mother had dropped down dead in the centre of Canterbury while out shopping. I well remember my initial reaction. She had looked perfectly healthy when she had see me off to school that morning. I could not believe that she had died as everyone that I knew who had died were either ill or old. I also recounted in chapter 13 that my maternal grandmother came to look after us, but then she died only one year and two days after my mother.
While recognising that we all have different personalities there are often reactions that are common in most bereavements.

Factors which can affect our grief
There are many factors that's can affect how we feel when someone close to us dies, such as the nature of our relationship with them, how reliant they were on us or us on them, and both their and our age at the time of their passing. The manner of their passing is another factor - whether their death was sudden and unexpected or due to a long drawn-out illness, or whether it was the result of an accident. It is particularly distressing if the accident was caused by a third party or deliberate violence. When a loved one chooses to take their own life, a whole range of added emotions and questions come. Maybe we could somehow have prevented them. If there was no warning, could we have spotted the signs? Different emotions coming to play depending upon whether the person was our parent, child, grandchild, sibling, grandparent, friend or other relative. It can also be difficult if our relationship with them had unresolved

conflict. Relationships can sometimes be complicated. Things may have been said that have caused pain or things that should have been said can no longer be spoken. The bereavement experienced by miscarriage or still birth is difficult, as there is grief over the fact that there was never a chance to get to know the child. In these circumstances, and also with the death of a child, it can have a negative impact on the parents' relationship, as each can sometimes get locked up in their own grief and be unable to support the other. Being bereaved can rock our whole world! Being bereaved can totally destabilize us! Nothing may seem safe or stable anymore!

We maybe someone who takes things for granted. Years have gone by and everything stays the same. We cannot imagine the people we love not being there, so it is a complete shock when the unexpected happens - or we maybe someone who has a tendency to worry so when the worst happens and our fears are realized, it sends as into a downward spiral. It has been stated that we never really get over the passing of someone we love. We just learn to live with it and get on with life, but the pain is always there underneath.

Some years ago, I remember watching a television documentary about the first world war. Several ladies in their nineties talked about their childhood. All their fathers has died in the war and each of them recalled the memory of the last time they had seen their fathers. Many decades has gone by, and maybe as time passed during the business of life, they had not spoken much about their fathers. But without exception, the tears roll down their faces as they relived that last memory of their father.

Expressing our grief

Sometimes our culture or upbringing can make us reluctant to show our pain by crying in public. We can feel it undignified and some of us can feel embarrassed and unsure how to react when we see someone upset. In Biblical times we see a different culture. Communities shared their grief. Paul, the apostle, in his letter to the Romans, urged them to "Weep with those who weep." The Ephesian church elders wept over Paul because they knew that they would not see his face again. Jesus, himself wept when he saw the outpouring of grief over Lazarus.

It is good that we share our grief. It can be an added sorrow to bereaved person when people avoid mentioning their loved one. We all want the memory of our loved one to live on and not to talk about them can feel like a denial that they have ever lived on this earth. We need to grieve and express our sorrow. If we bury our pain, we bury it alive and it can have a negative impacts on our future lives and relationships.

There are times in the grief journey when words are best left unspoken. I remember lovely Jewish lady called Tamar. She had two sons who both took their own lives while in the Israeli army. She told me that at times her grief would have been unbearable had it not been for friends in her church who would regularly just hold her while she wept.

Stages of grief

There are stages of grief that are generally universal. Many theories have been put forward on these stages. Some have said that there are four stages, some five or seven and some even eight! However, it is important for us to recognise that the edges of these stages can be blurred and we may experience many emotions all at once – and at times over the ensuing years. Some people look as if they are coping well at first, especially if they are very busy, but it may also be because they are in a state of shock. It can be much later when others might think that they should be recovering that they need a lot of support.

When a loved-one first dies, we may feel numb and almost can't believe it. Our mind finds it difficult to process what has happened. This can even be the case when we have known for sometime that the person is going to die, due to illness. We may feel that if we could only turn back the clock, they would still be with us. It hardly seems possible that this person who made such a big impact on our life is no longer here. If we have spent much of our lives looking after someone before they died, we can feel that we have "all this caring" in us that we don't know what to do with! On the other hand, it can be very difficult looking after an ill person for a long period of time and it is very understandable for conflicts to arise. Feelings of grief may be mixed with guilt and they may be made need to forgive oneself. After the initial shock of our loved-one's death, the awful realization dawns upon us that they will never be coming back. We can never again on this earth, hear their voice, feel their touch or see their face. We may experience all kinds of emotions. We may feel angry and feel it is unfair that our loved-one has died, particularly if their death was the result of an accident or sudden illness. We may blame someone for their death or even ourselves. We may feel guilty regarding issues that can now never be resolved.

As the reality of their death sinks in, the sorrow can be almost overwhelming and paralyzing. We may not feel like eating and sleep may elude us. If we do sleep, we wake up reliving what has happened.

Unresolved grief can make us physically and mentally ill. It is not unusual to experience seemingly unexplained physical symptoms and depression, but there are times when we just cannot accept our loved- one's passing and remain locked into our grief. If this state continues, our health is in danger and we really need to seek help.

As time passes, it is possible to continue with life and learn to live with our loved-one's absence, but still we can have moments of almost disbelief and sorrow at their passing especially at times when we would have loved to share an event or memory with them and particularly at birthdays, Christmas and other anniversaries. Finally, we accept what has happened, but we are not the same person as we were before our loss.

Nothing to live for!

After the funeral, life has to go on. It is sometimes difficult to imagine why everything seems the same when our world has fallen apart, and a person who was so central in our life is no longer on this earth. The pain bereavement can cause should not be underestimated.

I remember my grandfather's sorrow after losing my mother, his youngest daughter. He kept saying that children shouldn't go before their parents. Sometimes people can feel so bereft that they feel they have nothing to live for. They feel as if their hearts have been ripped out. My friend Jean's grief, when she lost her little boy, led to a suicide attempt.

When an older person dies, I have heard it said that we shouldn't grieve too much as they were old and we all have to go sometime. While there is some truth in this, it can be still devastating to those who loved them. For those who are widowed, it often comes at a time when they are older and vulnerable and less equipped to build a new life without their partner. I remember an elderly family friend who lost his wife saying that he found the evening so long. He wanted to share something with his wife but she was no longer there and his longing for her was intense. Although apparently in good health, it was not long before he joined her.

Children and loss

It has been said that children are very resilient, but I am not sure how true that is! Obviously, children all have different personalities and characters and can react in varying ways, but I believe that losing a parent or parents has a big impact on a child's life.

Many of us have heard Princes William and Harry speaking about their mother's death and the profound effect is has had on their lives and how they were only relatively recently addressing some of their issues. I recall seeing my grandfather the Christmas after my grandmother had died. I mentioned something about Christmas and my grandfather shouted at me, "How can you think about Christmas when your grandmother has just died?" I remember feeling so hurt and crushed, as I loved my grandmother passionately and was deeply affected by her death. Many years later when I was an adult and my father died just before Christmas, I was exactly the same as my grandfather and did not want to even think about Christmas. Children often react differently from adults, but it doesn't mean that they are not grieving or are unaffected, especially when it is a parent who dies, there was a big gap in their formative years.

Even when people lose their parents in later life it came prove devastating. When the second parent has gone, there is the difficult task of going through their possessions and maybe selling the family home. It can almost seem as if part of a life has gone with them as all those childhood memories which they played a central part in our life can no longer be shared with them. You are suddenly starkly aware that you are now the older generation!

Bereavement reminds us of our own mortality
When someone close to us dies, it can serve as a reminder of our own mortality and many people fear death. Although most choose not to dwell on it, for some it casts a shadow over their lives. In the Bible the writer of the letter to the Hebrews, wrote of how through Jesus' death and resurrection, Jesus overcame death for us and as we believe in him, we do not need to fear death. Verse 15 of chapter 2 states: --*also that He might deliver and completely set free all those who through the haunting fear of death were held in bondage throughout the whole course of their lives.* (Amplified Bible)
On the calendar, the day of my mother's passing, were these words:
The oriental shepherd walks ahead of the sheep.
It is tomorrow that fills men with dread!
Jesus is our Good Shepherds and He walks ahead of His sheep.
All our tomorrows have to pass Him before they get to us.

In memory of Edward Richardson 1998 – 2023
50% of the proceeds of this book will go towards bursaries for PGCE students at Durham University

www.ingramcontent.com/pod-product-compliance
Lightning Source LLC
LaVergne TN
LVHW051218070526
838200LV00064B/4957